THIRD EDITION

THE MEANING

OF SOCIOLOGY

Joel M. Charon

Moorhead State University
Moorhead, Minnesota

PRENTICE HALL

Englewood Cliffs, New Jersey 07632

Library of Congress Cataloging-in-Publication Data

CHARON, JOEL M., [date]
    The meaning of sociology / Joel M. Charon. —3rd ed.

    p. cm.
    Includes bibliographical references.
    ISBN 0-13-567512-X
    1. Sociology. I. Title.
HM51.C45   1990
301—dc20   89-37540
                                                  CIP
Editorial/production supervision and
    interior design: Shelly Kupperman
Cover design: Lundgren Graphics Ltd.
Manufacturing buyer: Carol Bystrom and Ed O'Dougherty
Cover: *Three Wise Men* by Wendell Brazeau. The Francine Seders

Gallery, Seattle, Washington. Photo: Chris Eden.

*I would like to dedicate this book
to Susan, Rose, Andrew, and Daniel.
They are the most important people in my
life.*

Printed in the United States of America

10 9 8 7 6 5 4 3 2 1

ISBN   0-13-567512-X

PRENTICE-HALL INTERNATIONAL (UK) LIMITED, *London*
PRENTICE-HALL OF AUSTRALIA PTY. LIMITED, *Sydney*
PRENTICE-HALL CANADA INC., *Toronto*
PRENTICE-HALL HISPANOAMERICANA, S.A., *Mexico*
PRENTICE-HALL OF INDIA PRIVATE LIMITED, *New Delhi*
PRENTICE-HALL OF JAPAN, INC., *Tokyo*
SIMON & SCHUSTER ASIA PTE. LTD., *Singapore*
EDITORA PRENTICE-HALL DO BRASIL, LTDA., *Rio de Janeiro*

Contents

PART TWO
THE NATURE OF THE SOCIAL ORGANIZATION

PART THREE
ORDER AND POWER IN SOCIAL ORGANIZATION

PART FOUR
THE DYNAMIC NATURE OF HUMAN SOCIAL LIFE

PART FIVE
CONCLUSION

Preface

Everything changes.

I change. Society changes. Sociology changes. The university changes. Students change. Therefore, this book must also change.

For better or worse, teaching in the university has changed over the past twenty years. It is easy for students to overlook important aspects of a university education, because they are busy trying to find a major that will help guarantee a secure future in an insecure world. It is easy to overlook *ideas*; it is easy to ignore the big questions about life that universities traditionally deal with.

This book is an introduction to sociology that emphasizes thinking about big questions: What is the human being? Why is our social nature so important? What is the relationship between the human being and society? Why is there inequality in the world? What causes change? This book examines all these questions.

Hopefully, when you finish this book you will feel as I do: Sociology is exciting, its questions are important, and its answers, although tentative, are useful.

There is a logic to the organization of this book. Part I, The Nature of Sociology, describes sociology as an academic discipline that takes a certain approach to understanding the world of the human being. This approach emphasizes our *social nature, social patterns*, and *socialization*.

Part II, The Nature of Social Organization, starts with the idea that we are *social*. We are *social actors*, we *interact socially*, and we form *social organization*. Social organization is made up of three patterns: *social structure, culture*, and *institutions*. The human being should be understood in the context of these patterns because in every organization, the human being is shaped and controlled to a great extent by these patterns.

Part III, Order and Power in Social Organization, focuses on two questions: How is *order* established in social organization? What is *social power*, and how does it operate in social organization?

Part IV, The Dynamic Nature of Human Social Life, describes *change*. Individuals change; society changes. Why? In this part of the book, there is an attempt to show that human beings make choices and are free actors to some extent. Although society does shape human beings, human beings, in turn, shape their own lives and therefore, human beings shape society. Although society does have patterns that have solidified over many years, there are always changes, and therefore what seemed inevitable to us as children no longer exists when we reach adulthood.

Part V, the Conclusion, briefly summarizes the ideas contained in the book and tries to answer the serious question that many students rightfully ask: *Why study sociology?*

Controversy characterizes the discipline of sociology. Because sociologists disagree on some very central issues, any attempt to write an unbiased introductory textbook can only be partly successful. Although some writers declare, "Our book is eclectic; it impartially describes all the of perspectives within sociology!" I have never found a truly eclectic book. This introductory book considers most of the different perspectives within sociology and is a mixture of these approaches as I understand them, but I am afraid that this book does have a bias. Read it as *one* introduction to the discipline, and realize that this is only a beginning toward an understanding of sociology.

In this third edition of the book significant changes have resulted from suggestions made by other professors and from my attempts to make the book clearer and more up-to-date. I am especially indebted to Professor Richard H. Hall, State University of New York-Albany; Professor David Olday, Moorhead State University; Joseph A. Blake, Indiana University East; Steve Manus, Alfred Publishing Company; Bill Webber, Prentice-Hall; and Nancy Roberts, Prentice-Hall. Denise Krause helped in the preparation of the manuscript.

Joel M. Charon

THE MEANING
OF SOCIOLOGY

Men and Girls Walking (1969) by Isabel Bishop. Aquatint on paper. The National Museum of Women in the Arts. Gift of Mr. and Mrs. Edward P. Levy. Reprinted with permission.

1

The Discipline of Sociology

I like understanding human beings. As a teenager, philosophy fascinated me. In college, history did. I majored in history simply because I was totally absorbed by questions about people and how we have developed the kind of world we have. I taught high school for a while, and there I dabbled in psychology, which, at the time, held great promise for unlocking mysteries concerning the human being.

I love music too, yet when I go to concerts I am sometimes more interested in the people there than in the music. What kind of person is the conductor? What is his or her relationship with the orchestra? How much conflict is there? Do they really enjoy practicing? Do they see each other as competitors for the top, or do they see each other as part of a team? Do they enjoy making music, or is it just a job for them?

I came to sociology late in my career. My first sociology class in college was not very interesting. I took the minimum required and never thought I would return. I barely understood what sociology was all about (something concerning social problems such as crime, alcoholism, and divorce), but I really did not take it very seriously. All I really knew was that it was something like psychology, so I was mildly attracted to it. Psychology studied the individual, I thought; sociology studied groups. I wasn't very sure we had to understand groups if we understood individuals.

Taking a class in social organization changed my whole view of sociology. As I listened to the instructor and as I read the material, a whole new world began to open up for me. I realized that sociology was a way of looking at the human being that I really never considered. We are, I was told, part of social organization, not sometimes, but all the time. This is our very central human quality. Everything is linked to this. I remember a student asking the instructor about freedom and social organization: If we are embedded in organization, then do we have free choice? That question has stayed with me to the present day. I also remember the instructor's answer (which I did not want to hear): Sociology is a highly deterministic perspective, one that sees much of what we do resulting *from* organization. From the sociological perspective, we are much less free than we think.

What happened to me was that I was more and more drawn into sociology. It became a passion for me. It offered explanations I had never encountered before. It never gave me final answers, but kept pointing out aspects of the human condition that I should consider if I was going to understand.

I have found that my early experience with sociology is not unique. Most people do not understand what it is. News commentators, psychologists, economists, high school teachers, and college administrators—many of whom have taken courses in sociology—generally do not have any idea of what sociology is. There are many stereotypes: We are social reformers, scientists in love with statistics, social workers, cold observers of human beings, testers of ideas that everyone knows. Most people seem to think of us as another version of psychology. I am even embarrassed to say that many sociology majors graduate with courses, with facts, with some ideas, but somehow without the ability to "think sociologically" about situations they encounter.

The purpose of this book is to give an introduction to the central ideas which make up the sociological perspective. Hopefully, you will come to understand it and see its usefulness. If it is any good you will see the world differently, and you will see yourself differently. Sociology has many facts and many specialized fields one can study; here the purpose is not to describe these, but to introduce the core ideas.

WHAT IS SOCIOLOGY?

Sociology Is an Academic Discipline

The university normally does not offer us certainty. If a university education works, we are left instead with a thirst for understanding more, and the humility to admit that we are not yet wise and all-knowing, and that if we are going to understand anything well, we must use care and control our tendency to be sloppy in our search.

The university introduces us to a number of *academic disciplines*. These are "academic" because they exist primarily in universities, and scholars there research and debate the knowledge gathered. These are "disciplines" because each has a long history, each has an accumulated body of knowledge, and each is a systematic and careful (hence, "disciplined") approach to developing ideas. Philosophy, psychology, sociology, history, physics, mathematics, and art, for example, are usually considered academic disciplines.

Each discipline has its own focus. Each then is a different *perspective*. Each examines a different aspect of reality. Each, by its very nature, tends to emphasize certain points and ignore others. Psychology examines the development of the individual, chemistry treats reality as a mixture of chemicals, and biology understands life as genes and environment. No single academic perspective can capture every aspect of reality or give us certainty, but a perspective can be a useful guide.

Sociology is *one academic discipline,* it is *one perspective* found in the university. Its history goes back to at least the nineteenth century (some would date it earlier than that). It has an accumulated body of knowledge, and over the years it has developed a systematic approach to understanding. For many, sociology is a very useful perspective. For some, it becomes a passion, for it constantly drives them to apply it to their world and to their own lives, and it truly alters their understanding in a very profound way.

Sociology Focuses on Our Social World

Sociology is one attempt to understand the human being. Its focus is on our social life. Typically, it does not focus on the individual's personality as the cause of behavior, but examines *social interaction, social patterns* (for example, roles, class, culture, power, conflict), and ongoing *socialization.* For example, sociologists examine the rules that develop as people interact, the expectations that arise among them, the truths that they come to share. Sociologists see the significance of the "student role," being "middle class," and being a "man" or a "woman" in modern American society. We notice how actors change as they shift groups or organizations, influenced by the inevitable socialization (attempts by people in the organization to form them) that comes with joining. Sociology begins with the idea then, that *humans are to be understood in the context of their social life, that we are social animals influenced by interaction, social patterns, and socialization.*

Most people are used to seeing the world psychologically, where action is thought to spring from the characteristics of the individual rather than from interaction and social patterns. From this perspective, people may explain the mass suicide of a religious cult as the result of religious fanaticism or a powerful leader or irrational and sick persons. Although this may be a partial explanation, sociologists perceive that a religious cult must also be understood as a society, as an organized group sharing a culture, as individuals influencing each other in interaction, as a structure with people filling positions and acting in accepted ways, conforming to each other's expectations, influenced by a power structure, as in any other group or society. As another example, instead of examining the characteristics of individuals who end up in prison, sociologists are more interested in factors relating to the positions these people have in society: how poverty "position" might influence criminal action, arrest, and imprisonment, or how power in society might influence how crime is defined in the first place.

Sociology Asks Three Questions

One way of understanding sociology is to recognize what holds the discipline together. In my view, it is held together, first of all, by its continuous attempt to answer three basic questions concerning the human being: What is the human being? What holds organization together? What are the causes and consequences of social inequality?

From its beginnings sociologists have sought to understand the nature of the human being. *What are we anyway?* Emile Durkheim, an important early French sociologist, described it well. Human beings are socialized into society. Society gets inside our very being. We take on society's rules, its morals, its truths, its values. In a sense, the individual becomes society. Charles Cooley and George Herbert Mead, two important American social scientists, emphasized that human beings are born unfinished: Human nature is learned, our very being results as we interact with others. That interaction continues throughout our lives, so we constantly change as we meet new people and take on new rules and new ideas. Throughout the history of the discipline, sociologists have uncovered a host of ways that human beings are, by their very nature, social, socialized, and forever changing in interaction.

What holds society together? What is the nature of order? Why are humans able to cooperate? This is the second concern of the discipline of sociology. Many call it "the problem of order." We are born into the world prepared to do very little. As we become socialized, we learn the ways of our society. Its ways become our ways, and that in part is how we begin to see how order is possible. However, it is far more complex than this. Order is developed through the social patterns we establish, through the rules, truths, and structure we create. It is maintained through families, media, schools, political leaders, and religion. Ritual, rules, punishment, and continuous interaction aid order. Karl Marx, another important early sociologist, showed the contribution of force and manipulation to order, and Max Weber examined the role of legitimate power, the willingness of people to obey authority. Much of sociology is an examination of the nature of order in society.

The third big question is also one that unites the discipline: *Why is there inequality in society and what are its consequences?* Is it inherent in the nature of organization? How does it arise? How is it perpetuated? What are the problems it brings, and how does it affect the individual? Marx saw inequality inherent in all class societies; Weber saw it inherent in the nature of lasting organization. Some sociologists see it as contributing to order; all see it as one source of social change. Sociologists are fascinated by the way inequality holds on and by the way it weaves itself through our lives. Many see it as the source of many of the injustices in our world; all see it as part of almost all social organization.

There are, of course, other questions that unite the discipline, but these three are the most basic ones. Examining these questions carefully should give you a good start at understanding what the discipline of sociology is all about.

Sociology Focuses on Five Topics

Thus far, we have emphasized that sociologists perceive the human being as social, and that they are interested in questions concerning the nature of the human being, the problem of social order, and the causes and consequences of social inequality. Sociologists differ from one another in which question they spend their time examining. They also differ in the topic area or focus they study. There are five topic areas:

1.   Some sociologists focus on *society*. Sociology to them is the "science of society." Society is that very large and abstract entity that humans exist in. Those who focus on society are sometimes called "macro-sociologists."

2.   A second focus or topic area is *social organization*. Sociology is the study of all social organization, from the largest unity—society—to the smallest—a pair of interacting individuals or dyad. Human beings live in organization: Studying the nature of all organization is a desirable goal.

3.   American sociology has typically become more specialized, and it tends to look at *institutions* or *institutional systems*. Some specialize in the family, some in schools, some in government. There is, for example, a sociology of law, criminal justice, health, religion, and military. Specialization has created experts who understand part of society better than the whole of society.

4.   Many sociologists are interested in the *micro* world of *face-to-face interaction*, how individuals act in relation to each other in everyday life. There is interest here in how individuals shape organization, how they share a view of the world, how they influence one another, how they are socialized in interaction.

5.   Finally, there is an emphasis among some sociologists on *social problems*, a concern about understanding poverty, family disorganization, child abuse, sexism, and racism, for example.

These five focuses, like the three questions, both divide sociology and unite it. On the one hand, sociologists differ in which question they are driven to answer, and they differ in which of the five general topic areas they concentrate on. On the other hand, most of us recognize that sociology is a combination of all of these, that together these constitute the outline of the discipline. Sociology might therefore be defined as *an academic discipline which examines the human being as social, a result of interaction, socialization, and social patterns. It is a perspective that concerns itself with the nature of the human being, the meaning and basis of social order, and the causes and consequences of social inequality. It focuses on society, social organization, social institutions, social interaction, and social problems.*

Sociology Is a Scientific Discipline

Some academic disciplines are sciences; some are not. From its beginning sociologists have regarded sociology as a science. However, what exactly does it mean to be a science? My goal here is to describe science by highlighting five principles.

First of all, *the purpose of science is to understand the universe in a careful, disciplined manner.* Although science is often used to change the world and solve problems, its first goal remains to understand. Science was developed because it was recognized long ago that casual observation of the universe is often misleading, and sometimes incorrect. Science tries to control personal bias and go beyond casual observation. To argue then that sociology is a science is to claim, first of all, that sociology is an attempt to understand the human being in a careful disciplined manner.

Second, *proof is the requirement for accepting ideas in science, and proof must be empirical.* The fact that someone who is intelligent tells you something is not good enough; the fact that experience confirms your opinion is not good enough; and the fact that you feel it intuitively may be good enough for you, but not for science. The ideas that characterize the field of sociology, and most of the ideas contained in this book, are ideas that have been slowly and carefully developed through accumulating evidence. That evidence must be empirical evidence. This simply means that evidence must be gathered through human senses. Normally, we mean by this that evidence is observed. Science is different from religion, which usually bases its ideas on faith, authority, and sometimes logical debate. It is also different from many nonscientific disciplines, such as philosophy and mathematics, which tend to base their ideas on good logic. Logic is part of the scientific approach, but scientists want more: *empirical observation as the basis for proof.* In sociology, therefore, as in all sciences, carefully developed tests are created—experiments, surveys, case studies, analysis of government data, for example—where results can be counted, observed, and shared with others who too are able to count and observe.

Third, science should be thought of as *a community of scholars, checking each others' work, criticizing, debating, and together slowly building a body of knowledge.* In sociology, as in all sciences, this community gets together at meetings to discuss research studies and publishes studies in professional journals and books for all to see and for all to learn, check out, and criticize.

Fourth, *science is an attempt to generalize.* Scientists attempt to go beyond the concrete situation and to establish ideas that relate to many situations. Scientists generalize about disease, gravity, animals, plants, stars, and people. In sociology we generalize about roles, minorities, revolutions, social change, class, social power, families, religion, and so on. People are part of nature. Although all things in nature are to some extent unique, if we are careful, we can intelligently generalize. Sociology is a careful attempt to make generalizations about the social aspects of human beings.

Fifth, *science is an attempt to explain events.* Good science is able to tell us *why things happen,* what the causes or influences on a certain class of events in nature are. So, for example, Weber showed how Protestantism was an influence on the development of capitalism, Durkheim showed how very low levels of social integration are an important cause of high suicide rates. Sociologists have explanations for (describe the influences on) crime, school success, change, and social conflict. They also are able to show the effects of racism, sexism, poverty, socialization, and role on other matters. *Science is an attempt to develop ideas about cause-effect relationships.*

From its beginnings sociology has claimed to be a science and to be guided by these five principles. There has been great diversity in how sociologists do science. It is rare, for example, to find laboratory experiments in sociology (or astronomy, for that matter). It has instead relied on experiments done by government or other organizations (affirmative action, busing, segregated education, Headstart, for example), on surveys, on real-life observation, and on carefully gathered data collected by various agencies and organizations. Sociologists try to generalize from historical documents. Sociology is a science of *diversity and creativity,* attempting to break away from simply accepting the traditional techniques borrowed from other sciences.

Max Weber's work represents to many the best approach to science in sociology.

1. Weber was a German sociologist who was faced with a

personal dilemma that he tried to resolve: Can a scientist be involved in the world of politics? Will involvement in politics sacrifice objectivity? Will devotion to objectivity be an excuse to avoid acting on important social issues? Weber resolved this conflict by arguing that sociology must be *value-free*—that is, every sociologist must self-consciously control his or her values in doing scientific work. We must see what *is* rather than what we would like to see. Weber did not mean that values can ever be perfectly controlled, but that must be our goal. He also maintained that as citizens sociologists should take stands: We should, for example, work for justice, equality, freedom, or whatever else we might favor, but as scientists, as observers of human beings, we must describe and explain, and that is all! Why believe us if we did not try to control our personal bias, as noble as it might be!

2. Weber also believed that science is a process of investigation, one that seeks truth but can never really attain it in any final sense. Although we try to control our bias, everything we do in scientific investigation—the kinds of questions we ask, the concepts we use, the techniques we set up—all influence what we find. Our truths therefore cannot be pure and cannot be final. Although this applies to all science, it especially applies to social science. Recognizing this, Weber called for a science which is open, where many methods are employed, many approaches taken, and different concepts used. He pointed out that scientists must be prepared in their own lifetimes to see their ideas replaced by others. To Weber science is not truth; it is an imperfect but often the best method for finding out something. It is frustrating to those of us who seek certainty!

Science is imperfect. All approaches to understanding the world are. Science focuses on cause, tends to ignore intuitive understandings, and accepts only that which can be established through empirical evidence—all of this, as useful as it might be, is, after all, only one way of understanding. Scientists sometimes get hung up on understanding trivial things which can be easily studied, and sometimes good creative ideas are discouraged. Sometimes scientific communities are not open, but are controlled by a few powerful scholars, and sometimes whoever pays for science controls what questions are investigated. Ethical questions also occasionally arise: the rights of people who are studied, the use of research by government or interest groups for purposes of distorting reality and defending policies.

The limits of science, however, must not cause us to ignore its importance for understanding reality. And the creative and diverse ways sociologists use science should not hide from us the fact that *sociology is a scientific approach to understanding the social life of the human being.*

The Meaning of Sociology: A Summary

Let us, for a moment, summarize here what sociology is. This chapter has described it as an academic discipline. It is one perspective. Its focus is on our social world, and it emphasizes that humans are social animals influenced by interaction, social patterns, and socialization. Sociologists are driven by questions about the nature of the human being, the problem of social order, and the causes and effects of social inequality. Sociologists study society, organization, social institutions, interaction, and social problems. Finally, sociology is a scientific discipline. It is one of those academic disciplines that takes a certain approach to understanding reality, an approach that emphasizes objectivity, proof, observation, a community of critics, generalization, and explanation.

THE BEGINNINGS OF SOCIOLOGY

People have not always asked the questions sociologists ask, nor have they gathered data about society as sociologists do. Sociology is really a late arrival to the university community and one of the youngest sciences. Although it is impossible to say, "*Here* is the beginning!" most sociologists find it convenient to place sociology's origins in the early nineteenth century with the work of a Frenchman named Auguste Comte (1798–1857), who was the first to use the term "sociology" and who defined sociology as the "science of society."

Like all perspectives, the development of sociology was linked to social conditions. After all, perspectives are ways of defining what is "out there," and not all societies encourage their members to examine society objectively and carefully. But nineteenth-century Europe was ripe for self-analysis. Several developments came together to bring about the right climate for the questioning spirit to grow and flourish. Let us briefly examine them.

Science Was an Inspiration...

Sociology was defined by Comte as the *science* of society, and it was indeed the development of science which was an important inspiration for early sociologists. Sociology grew out of a desire by some intellectuals to apply the techniques of science to the study of society. Before sociologists there were social philosophers, historians, political scientists, economists, and religious thinkers who looked at society or aspects of it. Most of these examined the political world primarily, and most were a mixture of understanding human society and searching for what human society should be. Often, objective investigation was not the goal.

Sociologists, however, took the advice of the Enlightenment thinkers of the eighteenth century: We can understand the laws of human society through applying the tools of science. Sociology from its start borrowed from the natural sciences the tools that were being used to fashion new discoveries about the stars, the earth, and the human body. The universe is made up of natural laws; so, too, society must be governed by such laws, and sociology would discover these laws through applying scientific procedures. Its purpose would be to describe what society is, not primarily to make a statement as to what it should be.

Sociology, then, was born in a time of intellectual excitement about the possibilities of discovery; indeed, Comte was so excited about the future of the science of society that he naively predicted that sociology (what he believed was the "queen" of all sciences) would be the focus of a new religion, and sociologists, as the bearers of knowledge, would be the "priests of the new order," moral leaders, solvers of the ills of humankind.

And So Were the Problems of Industrialization...

Not only was sociology born in a time of science, but also in a time when industrialization and urbanization were transforming the very basis of society. Some of the early sociologists saw industrialization as they saw science: a means by which the problems that plagued humanity would be banished. Poverty, disease, famine, even war would be ended. Other sociologists, such as Marx, reacted to the extremes of inequality and poverty that the Industrial Revolution telescoped, while still others, such as Durkheim and Weber, saw basic changes in the old patterns occurring, such as the declining importance of traditional religion and the growing bureaucratic organization of society.

In a real sense, sociology in the nineteenth and early twentieth centuries was an attempt by a number of thoughtful people to understand and clarify these profound changes taking place in society.

And the Need to Understand Revolution...

The French Revolution also exerted a powerful force on the development of sociology. The French Revolution was an unequalled social upheaval that began in 1789 and continued through the Napoleonic Wars ending in 1815, transforming the society of France and influencing all Europe and North America as well.

The intellectual community inherited that revolution: its ideals, its excesses, and the questions it posed. The debate of nineteenth-century Europe is still with us and influenced the beginning of sociology: Why do revolutions occur? What do they accomplish? How is order maintained in society and problems solved? How can a society deal with the excesses of inequality of power and privilege?

Sociology grew out of the twin concerns of inequality and order that the French Revolution inspired. Some of these early sociologists feared change; some welcomed it. Some wondered about the effects of declining tradition; some were amazed at how well the old held on. Some feared disorder; some hated inequality. All, however, were influenced by the memory of the French Revolution.

As Well as Experiences with Other Peoples and Societies

The new interest in society was also encouraged by "the march of empire"—the colonization of non-Western societies that followed centuries of discovery and exploration. As people learn about other societies, they may "be thankful we don't live like that," or they may come to see new alternatives of living never imagined; they may see opportunities to save those who are "less fortunate" or may decide that other peoples are inferior and incapable of profiting from the benefits of civilization.

In any case, thinking people are encouraged to examine their own societies from a new angle, are forced to compare, contrast, and seek answers to new questions about the nature of society in general. European intellectuals began this kind of examination when other lands were first discovered, but began in earnest as other societies became laboratories, places to explore rather than just conquer. Out of this development, too, sociology was born—out of an interest in society spurred by the realization that "things don't have to be this way; after all, look at the way others live."

And a Climate for New Ideas Arose

Along with the Industrial Revolution, the French Revolution, science, and the exploration of new lands, something else happened to encourage the development of sociology. European society was increasingly open to new ideas. This was a trend that went back a long time, but in a way the nineteenth century was ready for sociology, ready for a more critical, objective approach to society. If you think about it, this is not something that all societies can afford—scholars who spend time and money investigating an emotional issue like society, trying to control value judgments. Most societies probably would more appreciate scholars spending time describing society's many virtues. The freedom that accompanied the great revolutions of the late eighteenth and nineteenth centuries encouraged the development of all the social sciences. Sociology's time had come.

THE DEVELOPMENT OF SOCIOLOGY

Montesquieu, Saint Simon, Comte, and many others were the real beginnings of sociology. However, in the nineteenth and early twentieth centuries, four European thinkers were especially important to the discipline, and together could be called "the classical sociologists." They are Karl Marx, Max Weber, Emile Durkheim, and Georg Simmel. They exert an all-powerful influence to the present day: They are models for us, they inspire our ideas and studies, and their definitions of concepts are the places we still begin. By 1920 all had died, but together they left a strong sociological tradition in European universities.

The discipline of sociology came to the United States at the turn of the twentieth century. It quickly took on a distinctively American coloration, being imbued with a spirit of reform, and not at first distinguishable from social work. This spirit of reform has always been important to many American sociologists: an incentive for research for some, a subject of debate for others. American sociology has been strongly influenced by American pragmatism ("If it is to be worthwhile, show me how I can use it"), and right from the beginning it has had to deal with the problem of how to both understand society critically and objectively, yet attempt to reform it too. Although American sociology as a practical reforming discipline continues to be a variation, the dominant theme since these early years has been scientific understanding and explanation.

Between 1900 and 1920 sociologists increasingly put reform aside in order to gain respectability in the university and scientific communities. It worked to become a legitimate social science in major universities, especially in the midwestern and eastern United States.

After 1920 American sociology entered a period of both scientific theory and scientific research. Here was an attempt to build a discipline of specialization, accumulated scientific studies, ideas that had good evidence to back them up.

Also, after 1920 an important school (or perspective) in sociology developed in the United States known as *functionalism*. Up until the 1960s, functionalism was very influential, but since then its influence has declined. People influenced by this school have concerned themselves with the same issues as Durkheim—issues that focus on the problem of social order. Functionalists want to know how society works, how order is established, how the various parts of society—family, education, religion, law, and so on—function in society. There is an emphasis here on institutions, society's patterns, social organization, and social order. It is macro-sociology. Functionalism contributed much to the study of social organization in the United States but has become less and less important in the past thirty years.

Since the early 1960s sociology has gone in several directions. First, in the United States the scientific community has become increasingly specialized. Building on the research studies of previous decades, new ideas and empirical studies have divided the discipline into distinct fields: family sociology, sex roles, religion, health, bureaucracy, deviance, the military, government, social mobility, and so on. This is a predictable direction for any science, and there is every reason to believe that it will continue.

Second, a conflict sociology has emerged, concerned less with science and more with social issues, especially those related to inequality: class, poverty, sexism, racism, corporate power, white-collar crime, social conflict. Karl Marx, a nineteenth-century German thinker, and C. Wright Mills, a mid–twentieth-century American sociologist, are most influential in the development of this school. At first this school was called radical sociology, but by the 1980s it had clearly become a leading perspective in the discipline, had become broader in scope, and was associated with many who are less radical. Like the functionalist, the conflict sociologist tends to be a macro-sociologist. Conflict sociology is sometimes called critical sociology: It asks serious questions about society and about the direction of sociology—our loyalty to science, for example, our claim to objectivity, and our refusal to work for change. This conflict sociology has put forward a number of exciting ideas and studies and has become a vital alternative to the scientific specialists and functionalists.

Conflict sociology tends to be macro-sociology, focusing on the nature of society. The scientific specialists focus on societal institutions, often at the macro level, sometimes at the micro level. Interestingly, the late 1970s and early 1980s have seen the emergence of yet a third trend: an increasing interest in micro-sociology—face-to-face interaction, socialization, communication, the creation and maintenance of social patterns in small groups, presentation of self to others in situations, language, identity, roles, and so on. A number of schools have taken a micro-sociological approach. Historically, the most famous of these approaches is called the "symbolic interactionists," but increasingly important are the "ethnomethodologists," "dramaturgical sociologists," "phenomenologists," and "exchange sociologists." Together we might call this school the *interactionists*.

Specialization, conflict sociology, and interactionism are three important trends in the United States. Functionalists are far from unimportant, but their influence has declined since the 1960s. These trends (and others too numerous to describe here) make for disagreement and excitement within the discipline. Sociology is made up of people who honestly and seriously disagree with one another about many basic issues and about the direction we should go. We disagree about the nature of science and the nature of society. We disagree about focus and about concepts we should study. We disagree about the extent of inequality in society, the reasons for social change, the degree to which human beings are free within society, and the social problems that are most serious. Some are champions of Marx, while others consider Max Weber to be the model sociologist. Others regard Durkheim or Geroge Herbert Mead to be most useful, and still others are not interested in any big ideas while they do their empirical studies.

The excitement of sociology is that it is so alive with controversy and self-criticism. Ideas and studies are not taken for granted, since there are so many of us lying in wait to criticize. As in all science, such disagreement and criticism is necessary to assure that accumulated knowledge is accurate.

CONCLUSION AND SUMMARY

Of course, to those of us who work in the field, sociology is a very useful discipline. To many it is a passion, driving us to apply its ideas to every aspect of human existence.

To many outside the discipline, sociology is often misunderstood. Most people really do not understand the meaning of society and its importance to all that we do, are, and think. It is easier and more concrete to understand human beings from a biological or psychological perspective. Many people are not willing to accept a scientific study of social life, often because they do not understand science, and sometimes because they do not think we can generalize about human life.

To sociologists, however, it is very important to understand the human being carefully and objectively, using scientific principles wherever possible. Nothing is as fascinating as understanding why human beings act as they do, and nothing is as important.

Sociology, then, is an academic discipline that began in the nineteenth century. It is one perspective on the human being, and its focus is on our social life, on interaction, social patterns, and socialization. Sociologists are interested in the nature of the human being, social order, and social inequality. They examine society, social organization, institutions, interaction, and social problems. Sociology is a scientific discipline. Like other sciences it tries to be objective in how it studies the universe, it seeks to understand cause, it requires empirical evidence, it is an attempt to generalize, and it consists of a community of scholars who criticize and build on each other's work. Sociology began with the work of Auguste Comte, and it was inspired by the development of science, industrialization, the French Revolution, exposure to other societies, and a climate favorable to new ideas. The most important sociologists were Marx, Weber, Durkheim, and Simmel. In the United States sociology has gone in four different directions: functionalism, scientific specialization, conflict sociology, and interactionism or micro-sociology. Sociology is filled with disagreement and debate, but this is what makes it alive and exciting.

QUESTIONS TO CONSIDER

1. This chapter is an introduction to the discipline of sociology. Based on your understanding of it, how would you describe the discipline of sociology to someone who does not know what it is?
2. Based on this chapter, what are some of the ideas about human beings that sociologists believe?
3. Sociology claims to be a scientific discipline. What does this mean? Is it possible, in your opinion? What questions about the human being are beyond the scope of science? What are the strengths of science?

RECOMMENDED READING

The following works are good introductions to sociology as a discipline:

BABBIE, EARL. 1988. *The sociological spirit*. Belmont, Calif.: Wadsworth.
BERGER, PETER L. 1963. *Invitation to sociology*. New York: Doubleday.
BERGER, PETER L., and HANSFRIED KELLNER. 1981. *Sociology reinterpreted*. Garden City, N.Y.: Doubleday.
BOTTOMORE, TOM. 1987. *Sociology: A guide to problems and literature*. 3d ed. London: Allen & Unwin.
CHINOY, ELY, and JOHN P. HEWITT. 1975. *Sociological perspective*. 3d ed. New York: Random House.
GORDON, MILTON M. 1988. *The scope of sociology*. New York: Oxford University Press.
KENNEDY, ROBERT E., JR. 1989. *Life choices: Applying sociology*. New York: Holt.
LEE, ALFRED MCCLUNG. 1973. *Toward humanist sociology*. Englewood Cliffs, N.J.: Prentice-Hall.
MILLS, C. WRIGHT. 1959. *The sociological imagination*. New York: Oxford University Press.
SHIBUTANI, TAMOTSU. 1986. *Social processes: An introduction to sociology*. Berkeley: University of California Press.

The following works are good discussions of the lives and ideas of important sociologists:

COLLINS, RANDALL, and MICHAEL MAKOWSKY. 1989. *The discovery of society.* New York: Random House.
COSER, LEWIS A. 1977. *Masters of sociological thought.* 2d ed. New York: Harcourt Brace Jovanovich.
CUZZORT, R. P., and E. W. KING. 1976. *Humanity and modern social thought.* Hinsdale, Ill.: Dryden Press.
MARTINDALE, DON. 1960. *The nature and types of sociological theory.* Boston: Houghton Mifflin.
TIMASHEFF, NICHOLAS, and GEORGE THEODORSON. 1976. *Sociological theory.* New York: Random House.

The following are some excellent works by key sociologists:

DURKHEIM, EMILE. [1895] 1964. *The rules of the sociological method.* Trans. Sarah A. Solovay and John H. Mueller. Glencoe, Ill.: Free Press.
MARX, KARL, and FREDERICH ENGELS. [1848] 1963. *The communist manifesto.* Trans. Eden Paul and Cedar Paul. New York: Russell and Russell.
MEAD, GEORGE HERBERT. 1934. *Mind, self and society.* Chicago: University of Chicago Press.
WEBER, MAX. 1958. *From Max Weber.* Ed. and trans. Hans Gerth and C. Wright Mills. New York: Oxford University Press.

The following works are good discussions of sociology as a science:

BABBIE, E. R. 1982. *The practice of social research.* 3d ed. Belmont, Calif: Wadsworth.
BECKER, HOWARD S. 1977. Whose side are you on? *Journal of Social Problems* 14: 239–247.
COLE, S. 1976. *The sociological method.* 2d ed. Chicago: Rand McNally.
DURKHEIM, EMILE. [1895] 1964. *The rules of the sociological method.* Trans. Sarah A. Solovay and John H. Mueller. Glencoe, Ill.: Free Press.
GOULDNER, ALVIN W. 1968. The sociologist as partisan. *American Sociologist* 3: 103–116.
HAMMOND, PHILIP. 1964. *Sociologists at work.* New York: Basic Books.
HOROWITZ, IRVING L. 1967. *The rise and fall of Project Camelot.* Cambridge, Mass.: MIT Press.
LOFLAND, JOHN. 1976. *Doing social life.* New York: Wiley.
LUNDBERG, GEORGE. 1961. *Can science save us?* 2d Ed. New York: McKay.
MADGE, JOHN H. 1962. *The origins of scientific sociology.* New York: Free Press.
MILLS, C. WRIGHT. 1959. *The sociological imagination.* New York: Oxford University Press.
MYRDAL, GUNNAR. 1973. How scientific are the social sciences? *Bulletin of the Atomic Scientists* 29: 31–37.
WEBER, MAX. [1919] 1969. Science as a vocation. In *From Max Weber: Essays in sociology,* trans. and ed. H. H. Gerth and C. Wright Mills. New York: Oxford University Press.

The following are some good examples of scientific work in sociology:

BECKER, HOWARD. 1953. Becoming a marijuana user. *American Journal of Sociology* 59: 235–242.
BECKER, HOWARD S. 1961. *Boys in white.* Chicago: University of Chicago Press.
BECKER, HOWARD S. 1963. *Outsiders: Studies of the sociology of deviance.* New York: Free Press.

BLAU, PETER M. 1973. *The dynamics of bureaucracy.* 2d ed. Chicago: University of Chicago Press.

BLAU, PETER M., and OTIS DUDLEY DUNCAN. 1967. *The American occupational structure.* New York: Wiley.

DURKHEIM, EMILE. [1897] 1951. *Suicide.* Trans. and eds. John A. Spaulding and George Simpson. New York: Free Press.

ERIKSON, KAI. 1976. *Everything in its path.* New York: Simon and Schuster.

GOULDNER, ALVIN. 1954. *Patterns of industrial bureaucracy.* New York: Free Press.

HUNTER, FLOYD. 1953. *Community power structures.* Chapel Hill, N.C.: University of North Carolina Press.

KANTER, ROSABETH. 1977. *Men and women of the corporation.* New York: Basic Books.

LIEBOW, ELLIOT. 1967. *Tally's corner.* Boston: Little, Brown.

LIPSET, SEYMOUR MARTIN. 1956. *Union democracy.* Glencoe, Ill.: Free Press.

LOFLAND, JOHN. 1966. *Doomsday cult.* 2d ed. Englewood Cliffs, N.J.: Prentice-Hall.

LYND, ROBERT S., and HELEN M. LYND. 1929. *Middletown.* New York: Harcourt Brace Jovanovich.

MILLS, C. WRIGHT. 1956. *The power elite.* New York: Oxford University Press.

STOUFFER, SAMUEL A. 1949. *The American soldier.* Princeton, N.J.: Princeton University Press.

THOMAS, WILLIAM I., and FLORIAN ZNANIECKI. [1918] 1958. *The Polish peasant in Europe and America.* New York: Dover.

WALLERSTEIN, IMMANUEL. 1974. *The modern world system.* New York: Academic Press.

WEBER, MAX [1905] 1958. *The Protestant ethic and the spirit of capitalism.* Trans. Talcott Parsons. New York: Scribner's.

WHYTE, WILLIAM FOOTE. 1955. *Street corner society.* 2d ed. Chicago: University of Chicago Press.

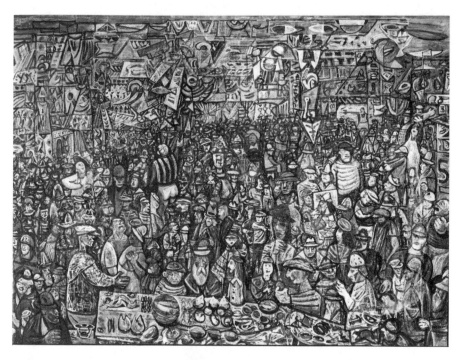

E Pluribus Unum (1942) by Mark Tobey, American (1890–1976).
Watercolor, tempera on paper mounted on panel. 19 ¾ x 27 ¼ inches.
Seattle Art Museum. Gift of Mrs. Thomas D. Stimson. Reprinted
by permission.

2

Sociology as a Perspective: How Sociologists Think

Chapter 1 is meant to be a general introduction to the discipline of sociology. This chapter is meant to introduce the way sociologists think about the human being.

The first question that unites sociology as a perspective is the question: What are we anyway? In this chapter we will begin to examine the answer to this question by looking at four topics within sociology that deal with it:

1. The social nature of the human being
2. The meaning and importance of social patterns
3. The meaning and importance of socialization
4. Durkheim's *Suicide: A Study in Sociology*

HUMANS ARE SOCIAL BEINGS

Probably the central idea in sociology from which everything else develops is that human beings are *social*. We live in society. Our lives are affected by one another. Dependence on others is a central fact of life. To be social does not mean that we necessarily like one another (some of us do not), but that without interaction and society human beings would be a different species of animal than they are.

Let us here be slightly more systematic. It seems that humans are social in at least six ways:

1. From the time we are born, we rely on others for survival. Our physical and emotional needs are met only through relying on others. It takes others to feed us and to protect us from danger. It also takes others to give us affection, feelings of worth, warmth, and love, all of which seem essential for growth. This is certainly true of infants and small children; it is probably true of people throughout their lives.

2. We learn how to survive from others. We do not know how to survive at birth. Instinct does not carry us very far. We learn how to get along in our world. Our actions are learned; they arise from interaction with others: parents, friends, teachers, television heroes, strangers, books. We learn how and when to fight, to work, and to have fun. We learn how to speak up, to keep from getting stepped on, and how to cook food. Life is learning how to solve problems that face us in our world. This is a lifelong process: We even must learn to survive when we retire, and we often learn how to die.

3. So we end up spending all of our lives in social organization. Every human being is born into a society, and rarely do we leave that society. We live our whole lives there. We live in an organized community, we work and play in many formal organizations and groups. Each one has rules for us to follow; each one socializes us; in many of them our lives take on meaning. Nature probably commands that we live our lives in organization or perish, but if nature does not command it, we learn it very early.

4. Many human qualities depend on our social life. Most religions define us as human because of a God-given soul. Governments recognize our humanity through laws that declare the individual as human at conception, at three months, at birth, or at another point in time. However, if we recognize central human qualities such as language, self, conscience, and mind as the basis for all human action, then at what point do we take these on? Whatever our potential for these qualities at birth, it clearly takes society to develop them. In a very basic sense, we become fully human through society. No stronger argument can be made for our social essence.

5. Many of our individual qualities depend on interaction. Each of us develops ideas, values, goals, interests, morals, talents, emotions, and tendencies to act in certain ways. These individual qualities are directed through interaction. Our society, community, family, and friends encourage some directions and discourage others. We are not perhaps exact copies of what others want us to be, but their expectations and teachings are important for our choices in life.

6. Finally, human beings are social actors. This means, like it or not, we constantly adjust our actions to others around us. Yes, we try to impress others some of the time, but we also try to communicate to others, we try to influence them, avoid them, or at the very least, adjust our acts so that we can do what we want without being bothered by them. However, because we live around other people, our acts are formed with them in mind, we are social actors, we must take their acts into account when we act. We do not live in isolation, so what others do matters to what we do.

The centrality of this social nature of the human being is where sociology begins.

Our social nature was not always appreciated, and many people do not appreciate its importance today. For a long time philosophers debated: What was the human being before society existed? Some argued that we were noble and good; others argued we were savage and evil. The sociologist has argued that *human beings are born into society*. Society precedes all of us. The first humans too were born into a society, with rules, people to socialize them, and so on. Without a society (however small it might be), we simply would not be human. We cannot conceive of the human being apart from society. Our nearest relatives in the animal kingdom depend on society too.

HUMANS EXIST WITHIN SOCIAL PATTERNS

The second idea that describes the sociological approach to understanding the human being concerns *social patterns*.

We are born into society. We live, we die. Society exists before we are born; it continues to exist after we die. But what exactly do we mean by "society"?

Long ago, Durkheim described society as made up of "social facts." By this he wanted to tell us that society exists "out there," an invisible but real force that works on all of us in some manner or another. Today, we sometimes call this "social forces" or "social patterns." Just as our biological inheritance influences what we do, so do these real forces that exist out there. Just as there is a physical and psychological reality, so too there is a *social reality,* a new additional force that emerges from the interaction of individuals. To say that something is *social* is to recognize that something real has happened *between individuals.*

Take rates, for example. Durkheim isolated suicide rates in society. Each society has a different suicide rate from every other society. In fact, these rates tend to stay stable from year to year. If they change, something else has changed and causes them to change. You and I are born into society; it has a suicide rate, a crime rate, a birth rate, and a death rate. We enter colleges that have drop-out rates, and we marry in a society that has a divorce rate. These rates are important to all of us. They exist as a force on us; their existence encourages or discourages our choices in life.

Social class as an example of social reality is even easier to understand. We are born into a class society. We are each located in that class system. We might be able to change our class, but our chances depend on the mobility rate. If we are born poor our chance for moving up is much less than if we are born middle class. What does class mean? It means that our lives are part of a social pattern that influences much of what we think and do. It influences our power, lifestyle, opportunities in life, with whom we interact, and the organizations which we join. Even if we do change class dramatically through luck, skill, and/or hard work, we will be subject to a new set of social forces operating on the new class position.

Culture is another important social pattern (or social fact). When we say that humans are cultural animals, we mean that society provides the individual with many ready-made answers to problems he or she will encounter in life. Many of our ideas exist in culture; we learn them and they become important to us. Many of our values and morals arise from that social force called culture. We do not develop in a social vacuum; our views are influenced by a social pattern that goes back a long time, often centuries.

Societies are made up of institutions too, and institutions are social facts that influence what we do. The fact that America is capitalistic, practices monogomy, and has a two-party political system makes a difference to all of us. Institutions are imperatives; they are developed patterns that direct all of us in our lives.

Most people do not readily recognize these patterns. After all, many argue, society is simply a conglomeration of individuals, and society is no more and no less than the people who make it up. Chemists, biologists, and psychologists do not usually bother with social patterns that are created among people, since their concern is with the individual organism and its development. The closest most of us come to recognizing the power of our social life is to admit that "other people influence us." The idea we have here called social patterns, social forces, or social facts is a much more complex and profound idea.

HUMANS ARE SOCIALIZED

To understand the sociological view of the human being is also to consider the concept sociologists call "socialization."

For society to function without serious conflict, the human being must be socialized. *Socialization* is the process by which the society, community, formal organization, or group teaches its members its ways. The family and school socialize the child, the fraternity must socialize its freshman recruits, the football team socializes its players, and society, in many direct and indirect ways, socializes its citizens. A socialized person is one who has been successfully made a member of his or her group, formal organization, community, and/or society. A socialized person controls himself or herself, but this self-control comes from learning society's controls.

Socialization creates the qualities that make us fully human. We have potential for human action at birth, but we take on language, self, mind, and conscience as we become socialized. What would we be like without socialization? Some adults are not very well socialized; they exhibit a lack of self-control, an inability to cooperate, a tendency toward impulsive behavior. There are very few examples of humans who developed completely apart from others, but all, when discovered, appeared very strange. It is almost impossible to imagine the human being without socialization.

The wild boy of Aveyron is probably the most famous case of a child who grew up without much human contact and therefore was not socialized. He was found roaming the woods and fields of Laune, France, in 1797. He was captured, turned over to governmental authorities, and studied by a number of scholars and physicians. He was about eleven or twelve years old, he did not have "the gift of speech," but instead used only "cries and inarticulate sounds." He rejected all clothing, he could not distinguish real objects from pictures and mirrored objects, and he did not weep. "He had no emotional ties, no sexual expression, no speech; he had a peculiar gait and would occasionally run on all fours" (Lane 1976,101).

Other cases of humans who grew up without social contact have appeared in the news occasionally. What emerges is a consistent picture: beings who do not use language, who react to others with fear and hostility, and who exhibit a general apathy. Cooperation with others becomes difficult, since human cooperation demands controlling oneself in relation to the whole, knowing what to do by understanding what others are doing, what George Herbert Mead called "taking the role of the generalized other."

Charles Cooley wrote that human nature does not come at birth. The human "cannot acquire it except through fellowship, and it decays in isolation" ([1909]1962,30). In a very real sense we are socialized to become human beings.

Durkheim captures well the meaning and the importance of socialization. Society, he wrote, is able to exist only because it gets inside the human being, shaping our inner life, creating our conscience, our ideas, our values. Society's rules become our own; its ways become ours. When people violate its rules, we are angered and we seek to reaffirm its rules through punishment. Because of socialization, when society's symbols—its flags, leaders, religious objects—enter our presence we are moved and we feel that we belong to something good. Because of socialization our identities become embedded in and dependent on society.

Marx, too, sensitizes us to the role of socialization in society. How is it possible to have a society where a few people own the means of production and control great wealth, while the masses must work for these few people and barely survive? Marx's answer is that the masses are taught to accept their place. They come to believe that they too might become wealthy if they work hard enough. They come to believe that the wealthy are somehow more deserving. They come to believe that this is the natural state of things, or that change is undesirable or impossible. Of course, Marx is at least partly right: Humans, no matter what position they have in society, are socialized to accept society, and if socialization works well, the job of the police is made much easier. Socialization allows society to get inside our very being.

Sociologists attempt to understand just how significant socialization is to every aspect of the actor. Human differences and similarities are understood in this context. Crime, success, values, morals, accomplishments, and failures are understood in part as resulting from socialization. Differences between men and women are located in socialization, as are differences in class and ethnic groups.

Of course, biology too may play some role. People have different potentials, talents, levels of "intelligence," and so on. Infants are in fact different from each other in temperament, size, looks, and sex. Yet immediately after birth they interact with other humans who encourage, discourage, and direct these various qualities. Sociologists want to know, therefore, what happens to the child growing up in poverty or in the upper class, how being male or female influences how others socialize us, and how different groups and societies handle different temperaments, looks, talents, and so on.

The social patterns described earlier are learned through socialization. We learn our positions and role expectations through socialization. We learn culture through socialization: what the organization thinks is true, worthwhile, and right. We learn our *identities*—who we think we are—through socialization. Even something as basic as *self-awareness,* our ability to look back on ourselves as objects in the world, comes to us through learning from others that we exist as entities. Others are our "looking glass," writes Cooley. Our self is our "looking glass self."

Socialization makes society possible. We are not like ants or bees: We are not born with instincts which direct us to cooperate. Instead, we are socialized to direct ourselves in relation to society. Without socialization, we would all be so different that there would be no possibility for cooperation or social order. Indeed, without socialization, we would act impulsively without any self-control. Self-control is social control, and social control arises from socialization.

Sociologists rightly see the concept of socialization as one of the central concepts in all sociology. It is a central part of our social nature and a good way to introduce the sociological perspective.

DURKHEIM: THE STUDY OF SUICIDE

Three points then, have been made in this chapter:

1. Human beings are social.
2. Human beings exist within and are influenced by social patterns.
3. Human beings are socialized.

Probably more than anyone else, the work of Emile Durkheim represents the perspective of sociology. Durkheim's intellectual life was spent making a place for sociology in the academic world. Before him, sociology was fighting hard for recognition in a world that revered psychology and biology. After him, it was generally recognized that human beings are social, affected by social patterns, and socialized. After him, it was also generally recognized that sociology was a science. Part of his success can be found in his most famous work, *Suicide: A Study in Sociology*. Let us look briefly at this work to see how Durkheim introduced to the world the outline of the science of society.

Durkheim was interested in studying suicide rates because he thought that such a study would help establish sociology as a scientific discipline. He wanted to show the importance of "social facts," his term for social patterns. Suicide, he argued, will always be a personal choice, and there are all kinds of psychological reasons one actor rather than another chooses it. However, even in this most individual of choices, social facts are at work—a society's suicide *rate* (high or low)—influencing the probability of an individual's suicide. This rate stays stable over time: We will find, for example, that one society might have 6 suicides per year for every 100,000 people, and another might have 12 suicides for every 100,000 people. This difference will hold true over a long period, so we might say that one society has a suicide rate twice as great as the other.

Durkheim's Theory

Durkheim was not interested in the cause of individual suicide. Why one person takes his or her own life and another does not is largely a psychological question. Taking one's own life is, of course, a very individual choice. However, even in the most individual of choices, social facts are at work—a society's suicide rate—and this social pattern affects what we do. If a society has a high suicide rate, more individuals will "choose" suicide than in one that has a low suicide rate.

However, what causes high or low suicide rates? Durkheim believed that the cause was another social fact, which he called "social solidarity," the degree to which a society is integrated, together, a solid whole. The opposite of high social solidarity is a high degree of individualism: If people are highly individualistic, then social solidarity is low. This is what modern times brings, he thought.

Low social solidarity (a social fact) will lead to a high suicide rate. Individualism will lead to greater reliance on self, less direction from and anchorage in group standards for guidance and meaning, with suicide becoming a more realistic option for many.

Durkheim's Evidence

Durkheim was a scientist. He wanted to test his idea carefully and systematically.

Durkheim had suicide data from government records for several European countries and provinces. He first divided these up between the Catholic and Protestant ones. He believed that because Protestantism emphasizes the individual's relationship to God and Catholicism emphasizes the Church as an integrated community worshipping together, the Protestant countries and provinces would have higher suicide rates. This is exactly what he found. The probability of suicide was significantly higher in Protestant than in Catholic communities. Durkheim's theory was supported, but not proved: There is not enough evidence here to conclude that social solidarity was the real influence. After all, perhaps Catholics have lower suicide rates than Protestants for reasons besides solidarity.

Durkheim continued to test his theory. He argued that if his theory was correct, then small communities (having higher social solidarity) would have lower suicide rates than cities. Examining his data, he found that this too was true. He went further: It follows, he reasoned, that married people would be more integrated into community than single people, women more than men, people with children more than people without, people who do not have a college education more than those who do (since college tends to break ties with groups and encourages individualism). Marriage, family, and lack of a college education is more likely to mean being part of a group, tradition, society; being single, without children, and having a college education discourages embeddedness in group, tradition, society. In every one of these cases he found that his theory was supported: single people, men, those without children, and those with a college education had higher suicide rates.

Durkheim kept going. How about the Jewish community? Will it have a high or low suicide rate? On the one hand, Jewish people in Europe were the most highly educated. On the other hand, their community was characterized by very high social solidarity. He found what he expected: The Jewish community had a lower rate of suicide than either the Protestants or Catholics. It is also easy to see why education did not make a big difference: Education took place *in the community,* and the purpose of education was to learn the traditions and ideas of the community. Instead of higher education encouraging individualism, it actually encouraged social solidarity.

What is the significance of this? Durkheim is doing several things at once. He is establishing the existence of social facts (social forces, social patterns), which influence individual action. We do not, it seems, make our decisions solely on the basis of individual personality factors; rather, our decisions are made in a larger social context, influenced by social forces we are not even aware of. Our society, if it is low on social solidarity, will influence more of us to choose suicide.

For his day, Durkheim's study is also good science. It shows how a scientist thinks and then tests his thinking creatively and systematically. Further, the study is published in a book for all of us to see. His data can be analyzed and/or criticized by others. We do not have to take Durkheim's word for either his conclusions or his evidence.

Durkheim Extended His Theory

Durkheim showed another characteristic of the good scientist. He added to his theory, showing that social solidarity has a much more complex relationship to the suicide rate. Where there is too little social solidarity, a high rate of *egoistic suicide* results. However, Durkheim also believed that *very high levels* of social solidarity also lead to high suicide rates, which he called *altruistic suicide.*

Altruistic suicide results from the fact that the individual comes to feel personal worth only through the group, gaining personal meaning only from something larger than self. Ego becomes nothing; giving up one's life to the society becomes honorable. Personal failure means that one lets down the group; dishonor and shame results, leading to high probability for suicide. Durkheim again tested his theory. This time he examined suicide rates in the army. The army has very high social solidarity; the army also has a high suicide rate. Within the army, career officers, volunteers, and oldtimers all had higher suicide rates than the others. If Durkheim had been alive during World War II, he would have pointed to Japanese kamikaze pilots and Japanese officers who lost important battles as examples of altruistic suicide. Probably the best modern example is the mass suicide at Jonestown in Guyana, where in November 1978 over 900 people committed suicide.

Durkheim's theory is interesting because it tells us that the relationship between social solidarity and suicide rates is *curvilinear,* that rates are higher at both ends of the scale in societies where there is either very high or very low levels of social solidarity.

Durkheim went further. He tried to isolate another social fact: the degree of change in society. This too, he argued, will affect the suicide rate. Societies that undergo rapid change will upset the social worlds of the individual, and the individual will find that the groups of which he or she is a part no longer give appropriate guides to action. The old standards no longer work, the individual will have to make more and more decisions on his or her own, with less and less anchorage in social life. Here Durkheim is not describing social solidarity, but whether one's society is an appropriate guide to the present. In times of rapid change the individual will reach a state of anomie, a term Durkheim used to mean without norms, without guides, a "state of normlessness." He appropriately called suicides that resulted from this state *anomic suicide.*

Durkheim again tested his idea. If his theory was right, then in periods of revolution, a society's suicide rate would go up. He found that it does. Also, he found higher suicide rates during times of economic depression and in times of rapid prosperity. He applied his idea to categories of people whose lives change suddenly: to those who become suddenly poor or suddenly rich, those who quickly become famous or drop into obscurity, who are released from pris-

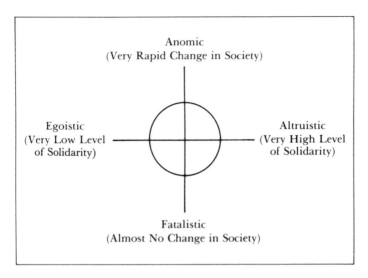

Anomic
(Very Rapid Change in Society)

Egoistic
(Very Low Level
of Solidarity)

Altruistic
(Very High Level
of Solidarity)

Fatalistic
(Almost No Change in Society)

FIGURE 2–1 The Conditions of Society Under Which Suicide Is Most Prevalent

oner-of-war camps, or who suddenly lose a close friend or family member.

To complete his theory Durkheim described a fourth type of suicide caused by too much control by society's norms. The extreme example is a slave society where life for the slave is characterized by too little change, too little hope for a better life, where the society is all-controlling, and where change is minimal. This type of suicide he called *fatalistic*. He did not test this idea beyond mentioning a few examples.

Figure 2–1 shows the four extremes of social change and social solidarity in Durkheim's theory. A society without any of these extremes will have the lowest suicide rate. Remember: What Durkheim is trying to do is to isolate social forces, or what he calls "social facts," and to show that these make a significant difference in our lives. We all live within a social context which includes a rate of social change, a level of social solidarity, and a suicide rate. What we do in our own personal lives is linked in many complex ways to this social context.

Durkheim's Influence

Durkheim's study of suicide has inspired much useful work. The concept of anomie has been applied to a number of theories and has inspired research in the area of deviance. Durkheim's study of suicide has influenced an important tradition in sociological research: that which uses careful statistical analysis for testing ideas. His study of suicide rates has opened doors to those of us interested in birth rates, death rates, divorce rates, and so on. He shows us all that science can be applied to an understanding of society, and he shows us the reality and the importance of social forces.

Durkheim's work encourages others. Many sociologists have taken his theory and applied it to their own society and their own times. His theory still works. We can test it today with data from the United States. Do the categories of people Durkheim predicted would have the highest rates still have the highest today? Single people? Men? Recently divorced? Recently widowed? Protestants? Urban? Based on what has occurred in American society over the past thirty years, which categories of people might we predict have rapidly rising rates? Jewish people (as they are less integrated into a Jewish community)? Women (as they become more independent and less integrated into family and community)?

His study has also inspired criticism, leading some sociologists to go in directions he did not pursue. Jack Douglas, for example, criticized Durkheim for ignoring how people perceive suicide, saying that the way groups of people think about suicide—how they define it—is more important than the abstract social facts of social solidarity and social change that Durkheim isolated. Others do not like his heavy use of statistics, and still others criticize the bias of governmental data.

Still, we have no better theory of suicide rates than Durkheim's. Although his data may not be as good as we would like, and although some of his thinking might not be consistent with modern standards, *Suicide* remains a lasting contribution to the field of sociology. And it represents very well three of the ideas contained in Chapters 1 and 2: Human beings are social, we live within social patterns, and sociology is a scientific discipline.

SOCIOLOGY: A SUMMARY

Suicide does not illustrate very well the central importance of socialization. Durkheim's other works do, especially *The Elementary Forms of Religious Life* and some of his essays on moral education.

Durkheim believed that society socializes its members to accept a common morality, what he called a "collective conscience." The acceptance of this is one of the prerequisites for any lasting society. Society's rules must become our own; its existence depends on our belief that its rules are right.

These first two chapters have introduced the discipline called sociology. Several ideas were presented:

1.   Sociology is an academic discipline that began in the nineteenth century. It is the study of the human being as a social being. It is a scientific discipline, and from its beginnings it has been characterized by disagreement and debate. These ideas were emphasized in Chapter 1.

2.   Sociology begins with the idea that human beings are social in very basic ways. We described six: relying on others for survival, learning how to survive, living our lives in organization, developing human qualities, developing our individual qualities, and being social actors.

3.   Sociologists emphasize that humans exist within social patterns, and that these patterns make a great difference to what we all do.

4.   Sociology is also the study of socialization, the process by which the individual learns the ways of society. There are many examples of the importance of socialization to what we all are.

5.   Durkheim's study, called *Suicide,* is an excellent example of much of what sociology is. It underscores the fact that we exist in society, that sociology can be a science, and that social patterns are in fact important to us.

It is time now to add meat to the skeleton. The next several chapters will build on these first two, and they will show the many ways in which the individual and society are intimately linked.

QUESTIONS TO CONSIDER

1.   Human beings are social by their very nature. Can you explain this? Do you agree with it?

2.   Human beings exist within social patterns. Can you explain this? Do you agree with it?

3.   Human beings are socialized. Can you explain this? Do you agree with it?

4.   Explain to someone the basic idea contained in Durkheim's *Suicide.*

5.   Suppose you were interested in testing Durkheim's theory of suicide today. What populations would you choose to study?

RECOMMENDED READING

The following works are good discussions of the social nature of the human being:

BERGER, PETER L. 1963. *Invitation to sociology.* New York: Doubleday.

BERGER, PETER L., and THOMAS LUCKMANN. 1966. *The social construction of reality.* Garden City, N.Y.: Doubleday.

COOLEY, CHARLES HORTON. [1902] 1964. *Human nature and the social order.* New York: Schocken Books.

COOLEY, CHARLES HORTON. [1909] 1962. *Social organization.* New York: Schocken Books.

DOUGLAS, JACK. 1967. *The social meanings of suicide.* Princeton, N.J.: Princeton University Press.

DURKHEIM, EMILE. [1895] 1964. *The rules of the sociological method.* Trans. Sarah A. Solovay and John H. Mueller. Glencoe, Ill.: Free Press.

DURKHEIM, EMILE. [1897] 1951. *Suicide.* Trans. and eds. John A. Spaulding and George Simpson. New York: Free Press.

DURKHEIM, EMILE. [1915] 1954. *The elementary forms of religious life.* Trans. Joseph Swain. Glencoe, Ill.: Free Press.

ELKIN, FREDERICK, and GERALD HANDEL. 1978. *The child and society.* 3d ed. New York: Random House.

HARRIS, MARVIN, and EDWARD WILSON. 1978. Heredity vs. culture: A debate. *Society* 15 (6): 60–63.

LANE, HARLAN. 1976. *The wild boy of Aveyron.* Cambridge, Mass.: Harvard University Press.

MCCALL, GEORGE J., and J. L. SIMMONS. 1978. *Identities and interactions.* New York: Free Press.

MERTON, ROBERT K. 1968. *Social theory and social structure.* New York: Free Press.

MILLS, C. WRIGHT. 1959. *The sociological imagination.* New York: Oxford University Press.

SECORD, PAUL F., and CARL W. BACHMAN. 1976. *Understanding social life: An introduction to social psychology.* New York: McGraw-Hill.

SHIBUTANI, TAMOTSU. 1961. *Society and personality.* Englewood Cliffs, N.J.: Prentice-Hall.

Seed for Sowing Shall Not Be Milled (1942) by Kathe Kollwitz,
(1867–1945). Lithograph on ivory wove paper. Galerie St. Etienne,
New York. Reprinted with permission.

3

Humans Are Embedded in Social Organization

We hear words like *group, organization,* and *society* all the time. Most of us have some notion as to what they mean. The purpose of this chapter will be to try to define these carefully and show their usefulness in the perspective of sociology.

To say *organization* is to say *routine, pattern, continuity.* Let's get organized! really means let's put things into place, let's have some order, let's establish a pattern that we can all use, let's get together so we know what each person is doing. That is the basic meaning of organization: *the patterns that develop among people over time.* Sociologists study these patterns, how they are created, and how they come to influence, direct, or control the actors—ourselves.

Almost every person is born into social organization. Many of the social patterns that we discover in our family, community, and society have been developed long before we enter them. Characteristically, individuals become part of social organization and are subject to its patterns. Only once in a while do they participate in creating social organization.

Where do social patterns come from? How do they arise in the first place? How are they reaffirmed? Altered? Done away with? The simplest answer is *interaction.* As people interact they develop social patterns—organization. Where interaction stops, social patterns die out. Where interaction is segregated, more than one organization develops. Where interaction is interrupted, where many new actors enter in, where new problems arise for those in interaction, the social patterns are altered.

Interaction is the key to understanding social organization. The key to understanding interaction is *social action,* to which we shall now turn.

ORGANIZATION BEGINS WITH SOCIAL ACTION

We all act—that is, we do things, we exhibit movement toward the world around us. Indeed, to fail to act is to be dead. Max Weber argued that the best way to define the subject matter of sociology is as the study of one kind of action—social action. Of course, humans are not only social actors, but social action dominates much of what we do. It is central to understanding what human beings are.

Social action had a special meaning to Weber. For some people, *social* means being a lot of fun at parties, "socializing," being friendly, being nice to others. Others recognize that *social* has something to do with groups and society, that individual action is somehow influenced by other people. Weber, too, argued that humans are influenced by other people, but his analysis went beyond this.

Social action, according to Weber ([1922] 1957) takes place when the actor "orients his acts" to others and is thus influenced by them: The actor takes account of others, acts for others and in spite of others. The actor acts to influence others, to communicate with them, to affect them, or to do all the various things people do with others. *Where others make a difference to what we do, where we think of others as we act, there is social action!*

Examples are everywhere. In a sense I am writing this sentence for an audience even though there is no one in the room with me. When I see you and say "Hi!" my speech is aimed at you and it is therefore a social act. When you turn your head and keep walking, ignoring me, you are also acting for me. When I talk to you, whistle, give you the peace sign, hit you, embrace you, hold your hand, sing to you, throw a baseball to you, I am engaging in social action. But also when I dress in the morning and imagine what I will look like to others, this is social action. When I move off into a corner so I can escape being noticed at a party, I am a social actor since others in the situation make a difference to what I do. When I conform so I do not look like a fool to others and when I refuse to conform and tell others they are the fools, I am a social actor.

The key to social action is *acting with others in mind.* All intentional communication is social action, but communication is not essential to social action. (If I am a thief, I will act with police in mind so I do not get caught, yet I do not necessarily wish to communicate anything.) Sometimes the people we have in mind are part of our current lives; sometimes they are part of our past (people we know who have died) or our future (future generations of Americans); and sometimes they are even imagined (I am writing this book for an imagined audience). Sometimes we act with an individual in mind; sometimes with a group (our friends) or even a society (the United States).

Not all action is social action. If it is raining and I put up my umbrella, I am obviously not acting for the benefit of anyone but myself. Even if someone else puts an umbrella up and I see it and do the same, that is not social action either; it is imitation. It is only when I open up my umbrella in part for others, for an audience, that it becomes social. If it is pouring, and others look at me holding an umbrella in my hand, and I decide that I had better open it up so they do not consider me a fool, my act becomes a social act. Or if I offer to share it with the person next to me who is getting soaked the act becomes social.

Social action is *intentional action.* I think of others as I act, I intend my acts for others, or I at least take account of others. This means that actions that are purely emotional or habitual would not be social actions. Of course, there are probably no purely emotional unthinking acts, since even in our most emotional moments, we act with others in mind to some extent. If I bang my head on a doorpost and take my anger out on a friend by yelling at him, my act is not primarily a thinking one and it is not significantly social; yet there is at least a small element of thought in my act and it is certainly oriented to another person, so it is social to some extent. And when I do something habitually and I do not carefully consider anyone else in the situation, there is also an exception to social action. But this, too, is quite rare, since most situations demand that we take into account other people. Driving may be habitual, but hopefully it is also social since every situation must take account of other drivers. So almost all of our actions, even emotional and habitual responses, have an element of "taking others into account." We are almost always social actors.

Social action is important to what we are. We live our lives around others, and these others come to make a difference to what we do because we often *have to consider them.* Therefore, what we do at any moment is to some extent shaped by the *situation,* by the presence of particular others. Our action then changes as our audience changes. I will act differently depending on who I am acting for at the moment. Sometimes my parents, my friends, a professor, a clerk, or a class of students will be my audience, and I will be influenced by their presence. It is not that we are only trying to impress each other—although this is a part of it—but we are also trying to influence each other, to communicate, to love, to manipulate each other, and what we do depends on what is appropriate in the situation we find ourselves in. *Social action, then, means that humans adjust from situation to situation*—not drastically, perhaps, but we change nevertheless. And when we stay the same it is generally because our audience has also stayed the same. What we do is largely dependent on the particular social world we are acting in. The importance of social action to what we are underlines once again the fact that we are social beings.

MUTUAL SOCIAL ACTION IS SOCIAL INTERACTION

Much of what humans do results from their interaction. Sometimes I take you into account when I act and you take me into account when you act. The presence of each makes a difference for the other's acts. This is *mutual social action* or simply *social interaction. Social interaction is when each person is both subject and object; that is, each person acts toward the others, and is in turn considered an object by the others.* The presence of each and the actions of each make a difference to the others' actions. This happens between you and me when I ask you to dance and you say no! It also happens when you say yes, when we walk onto the dance floor (keeping each other in mind), when we dance (unless we imagine only the audience around us or we respond only to the music and not each other), and also when we sit down for a drink. And we can imagine the many ways that interaction might take place through the evening, start again the next week, continue for a whole year or even for a lifetime.

Some social action never becomes interaction, some interaction lasts only for a second, and some continues over time.

Sometimes we act toward each other and do not understand what the other is really intending by his or her act. I act to impress you; you think I'm being foolish. You laugh at me and I interpret your laughter as an interest in me. We continue to misunderstand each other's actions and intentions, and our interaction might lead to conflict or to a quick end to the relationship. We can correct each other's interpretation and interaction will continue.

Interaction occurs between and among people. It is not person A plus person B, but what happens as A and B act toward each other. Action cannot be predicted simply by knowing *who* the actors are; action unfolds over time as each takes into account the presence and the actions of the others.

An instructor begins a lecture. A student asks a question. The instructor now alters what she intended to do in the lecture. She backs up and repeats what was said the day before. Another student becomes confused and asks a question. No one intended the class to go in this direction, but it does: The social acts of various actors direct the flow of action. So it is in conversations, buying and selling, playing chess or cards, driving a car, fights, sexual encounters, and any action that involves others. What we do becomes an important consideration for others; what they do becomes an important consideration for us. No one can fully control a social situation.

Clearly, *interaction is very important as a cause for human action.* Actors adjust to each other, and are thus affected by each other's acts. As interaction unfolds plans are altered, actions are evaluated, altered, and aligned. People find themselves doing things they never imagined they could or would do, simply because the interaction leads them to a certain point. We are all potentially saints or sinners, and we become either or both depending in part on our interaction.

Interaction is also very important because it is the source of our socialization. To some extent, every time we interact we are being socialized. Interaction forms what we are—gives us new ideas; poses new options; influences our values, self-image, identity, attitudes, and general personality. We are formed, reaffirmed, and altered as we interact. We learn to steal in interaction; we learn to value school in interaction. We learn that we are intelligent or beautiful in interaction; we learn prejudice or openness in interaction. We become a traditional woman or a feminist in interaction; we become religious, patriotic, or revolutionary in interaction. To some extent at least, we become a problem drinker or drug abuser in interaction; and to some extent we break our addiction through interaction.

Interaction leads to social patterns. It is the very basis for all social organization. Imagine what happens in interaction over time. We develop relationships. We know more and more about what to expect from each other; we come to understand more clearly each other's meanings and intentions; we come to agree on a number of matters; we come to develop routines of action; and we are less and less surprised by each other's actions. We have developed *social patterns* or *organization.* Social organization, then, arises from interaction.

SOCIAL ORGANIZATION IS PATTERNED SOCIAL INTERACTION

Patterned social interaction is what sociologists call interaction in which action becomes more organized, less spontaneous, less accidental or different, and we come to know what others will do and what we are supposed to do in relation to them. We do not have to start over, we do not have to explore how to act with each other whenever we come together. We have not necessarily changed as individuals, but we have changed around each other. We have entered into interaction with rules.

Patterns are more than the individuals who make them up; they are like new, additional forces that have arisen among people and now exert influence on each individual. They are not explainable just by adding up the individuals involved; they are social facts above and beyond the individuals themselves. Thus when people interact over time they are influenced not only by each other's specific acts but also by the patterns that are developed among them. A boy and a girl who date are influenced not only by each other, but by the rules and the ideas they have both come to accept in the relationship; no outside dating, an openness in sharing personal problems, casual dress, a certain kind of humor, a sharing of dating costs, a right mixture of seriousness and humor in situations, a certain code of behavior around parents, adults, friends, employers, and other people whom they know personally.

Patterns are even more obvious when there are more than two people interacting over time. A family which includes children must develop patterns so that the three or four or more will know what to expect from each other when they are together. Sometimes the patterns are even written down: A marriage ceremony is an attempt to do this (especially when the couple writes its own ceremony), and the army is a good example of what seems to be millions of patterns written down, amended, amended again, and superseded. Interaction develops patterns that individuals easily recognize and, on the whole, follow. Patterns allow interaction to continue with less and less difficulty, so that each individual knows what to expect from the others and knows how to act in relation to others. Patterns take the guesswork out of interaction. Patterns are not all that exciting, they do not bring surprise or novelty or marvel, but they are important for helping us through the day without making us think very hard about every situation. Patterns bring organization, consistency, stability, and routine to our everyday existence. Without social patterns, cooperation on an ongoing basis would be impossible.

Most of the time the social patterns that we follow have been established by others who have interacted and developed the patterns. We enter the interaction, learn the patterns, and do what we are supposed to do. We know how to act in a movie theater because the patterns have been established, and parents or friends taught us what to do in such places. Teachers establish rules and students are taught them the first day of class. Indeed, if they are not clear, we ask. We are born into families whose patterns are already formed to a great extent, and when we enter a fraternity, a business, a grocery store, or a new job, we have little if anything to say about the patterns we follow. A *society* is a social organization that has existed for a long time, and the social patterns we live by we are born into and normally accept as part of our taken-for-granted world.

Start up a softball team. The game of softball has social patterns you inherit: positions on the team, a body of rules, and even the right ways to field ground balls, catch flies, and bat. The league you join also has social patterns—rules, schedule, places to play—that others have developed for you. The team might develop its own social patterns as to how matters are decided—for example, who plays where, who bats when, how the captain is chosen—but there is not great room for originality. Playing together establishes social patterns, in that people know what to expect from each other in the outfield, infield, and so on. As such, matters are "set," they become social patterns that all follow so that there can be a cooperative team. New situations arise; old rules are applied. "That's not fair," is often the cry of an individual who feels that a social pattern is being violated. Once developed, social patterns take on a life of their own. "That's just how we do things around here. If you don't like it, it's tough." And when the umpire steps onto the field, hundreds of additional rules now govern the team.

In summary, we have emphasized that our social life influences what we all do:

1. We are social actors. When we act, we take others into account—they matter for what we do.

2. We interact, and interaction influences the flow of action on each actor's part, it socializes us, and it leads to social patterns.

3. We develop social patterns through interaction with others—these patterns then exert themselves on us as we continue in the interaction.

4. Most situations we enter have patterns already set for us which we learn— and these patterns influence what we do.

THE FORMS OF SOCIAL ORGANIZATION ARE DIVERSE

Imagine social organization, then, as interaction plus patterns. A committee, a corporation, and a society are "organized" or "patterned social interaction." Such organizations take five forms: dyads, groups, formal organizations, communities, and societies. All are the same in a very basic sense: Actors interact with each other on a regular basis far more regularly than they interact with outsiders, and that interaction has developed social patterns that significantly influence their lives.

Dyads Are Twos

Dyads are formed when there is patterned social interaction between two people over time: friends, lovers, doctor-patient, mother-son, husband-wife. The patterns come into play whenever the two people interact, whether face-to-face or apart (as by letter or telephone).

Groups Are More

The most common word used to refer to numbers of people is *group*. In sociology a group is not just a number of people who are alike (such as people with blonde hair or people who live on Third Street), but a group, like a dyad, is made up of people who interact and form patterns. A group, however, is made up of three or more individuals.

When the individuals get together they act according to the patterns. We may smoke all we want when we are with Helen and Edith, but when we are with Martha and Mary we know that smoking is out. We talk up a storm around our friends, but we keep quiet in class. I remember how important it was in my junior high days to be "cool" at parties with mixed (boy-girl) company, and how silly I acted when I was with George and Dave, and how serious I was in my interaction with Mike. In my family I kept quiet, and when I was with my brother alone I had to establish my superiority. In each group and dyad the patterns were different, I knew what they were, and I adjusted my action accordingly. I'm not unique—we all do this it seems.

Groups are everywhere. A family is a group (dinner at six, mom and dad get to sleep until ten Saturday mornings, children's rooms are their territory not to be violated, no fighting in public, church on Sunday, drinking is all right sometimes, mom makes decisions about money); the gang that gets together at Louie's Cafe Thursday night is a group, as is the Sunday afternoon baseball team and the committee appointed by the Chamber of Commerce or by the student senate. These are all examples of groups that are continuous and last a fairly long time. The patterns become taken for granted, and we are most aware of them when someone decides to violate them.

Often, however, dyads and groups exist for no more than a few minutes or perhaps an hour, a day, or an evening. When people gather at a party they form a group (indeed, there are probably several groups formed), which changes as new people come in and others leave. These short-lived groups are still groups; there is interaction (mutual social action) and patterns emerge. The patterns are simple and slight at first, but after several minutes or an hour more and more understanding about what one is to do and how the others see our acts is shared and affects all participants. And the more the group becomes isolated from other groups, the more its patterns become established and unique. Some sociologists have done extensive research on small-group discussions and have discovered that patterns emerge very early and remain fairly stable over time.

At first glance there may not appear to be much of a difference between a dyad and a group, but size does indeed affect the nature of the patterns. Georg Simmel (1858–1918), a famous German sociologist, analyzed how dyads and groups differ:

1.   In a dyad there is instability and insecurity not characteristic of the group, for the dyad is faced with dissolution if one person leaves. A group is capable of survival if a member leaves or is replaced, since it has a "collective identity," which does not depend on any one individual.

2.   In a dyad, an individual can veto collective action. In a group the individual, if he or she wants to remain in the group, may have to do things contrary to desire, since the possibility exists that he or she will be outvoted. No longer does the individual have the power to veto action.

3.   A dyad cannot have a coalition (an alliance), but in groups coalitions will inevitably occur, and this makes the group qualitatively different from the dyad. Such coalitions can be predicted beforehand. According to the work of Theodore Caplow, for example, in the triad (three-member group), the two weaker members will usually try to balance the power of the strongest.

4.   Dyads are usually more intense, exhibit more emotional involvement, and are less impersonal than groups.

One more difference is implied in Simmel's discussion. The third party brings a "collective unity" not evident in the dyad. This has something important to say about social patterns, the central topic of this chapter. Although the dyad develops its own patterns, it is only when a third party enters that the patterns become truly independent of the actors. Although patterns are developed in dyads, and although they influence action, only in the group do they take on a life of their own, apart from the actors who create them. This is one reason why dyads, more insecure, more personal, and less dependent on social patterns, will try to add a third force to the relationship: a ring, a child, a treaty, a written vow.

Most of us are members of a wide variety of groups. We are born into a family group, we form friendship groups, we learn in a schoolroom which is made up of one, and often several, groups. We work in groups, we play in groups, and we are socialized in groups. We discuss our concerns in groups, and it is in groups that we test out our ideas about the world and we come to share perspectives about the world.

Certain groups Charles Cooley (1909) called *"primary groups."* These are groups that are *small, relatively permanent, intimate, and unspecialized.* Individuals feel a close attachment to such groups, and they fulfill a wide range of personal needs. Cooley called these primary because they are *important to both the individual and the society.* These are the groups from which individuals receive their early socialization, and thus they are the ones that are most responsible for imparting those qualities that make us all human: language, self, mind, conscience. They provide individuals with close emotional ties important for general well-being. Such groups also are important for society, for they influence individuals to see the world as those in society do and to control themselves as those in society wish.

Of course, many groups in modern society are not primary; indeed, increasingly our groups tend to become larger, temporary, impersonal, and specialized. Such groups are called *secondary.* A business organization is a secondary group, a college class is, and so too are most of the social clubs to which people belong. Our religious, educational, and leisure time activities are filled with examples of groups that are secondary. Often secondary groups become so large and complex that their social patterns must be made very explicit, often in written form. Such groups are called *formal organizations,* the third form of social organization.

Formal Organizations Write Down Their Rules

As groups become larger they generally become more formal and impersonal; patterns are made more explicit and are formally stated, so that members clearly understand what is expected. Face-to-face interaction occurs but less predictably; if patterns are to continue they must depend on more than continuous interaction. *When a group makes patterns explicit through writing down rules, it becomes a formal organization.*

A formal organization may be small, but usually it is large. It is difficult for large numbers of people to know how to deal with each other in an orderly way without some written guidelines. Sometimes a dyad becomes a formal organization in order to establish itself on a more secure level—for example, through a blood pact, a marriage or business contract—but usually it is characteristic of a larger group—a fraternity, a business corporation, a college, the army, the state department. Formal organizations characterize modern society—everything is written down, we rely on rules that can be read. Our relationships are impersonal to a great extent, organizations are large, and we are often one small actor in a very large formal organization where not many people know our name, but where people know us by the positions we fill.

Interestingly, formal organizations inevitably inspire the formation of informal patterns which often become more important than the formal. The way things are supposed to be on paper is balanced by patterns that actors negotiate on their own in face-to-face interaction. Formality aids people when they interact—it makes it relatively easy for new members to know very quickly what to do—but it is usually more important to alter the written patterns and bend them to fit our own situation, since those who wrote them could not possibly know our situation exactly. Indeed, most people in formal organizations seem to understand that written rules are guides that are not usually strictly adhered to. Sometimes a problem occurs when it is not clear to actors to what extent the formal patterns are to be followed. Doctors know what they should do in hospitals; nurses know what they can do. But the formal rules are often bent because the real situation demands negotiated patterns; the doctor's lack of time, the nurse's willingness to take responsibility, and the patterns negotiated between them become more important than the formal rules. On the other hand, as suits against doctors and hospitals increase, formal rules take on even greater importance, since following them helps protect people in courts of law.

Communities Are Self-Sufficient Units of Organization

Sometimes the group or formal organization becomes relatively self-sufficient or independent of other social organizations. It takes care of the basic needs of its members—economic, social, cultural, education, political. People are able to live their whole lives within this social organization, carry out most of their activities within it, and only occasionally leave it. This is called a *community,* and it is the fourth form of social organization.

A family could be a community if its members interact primarily with each other in the basic activities of life—if, for example, it produces its own food, it supplies the leisure-time activities of its members, and it takes care of its members' health and education. Usually, however, the family is located in a larger community—a Hutterite settlement, Baudette, Minnesota, New York City. Harlem is a community within New York City, and a commune in Virginia is also a community. A prison is a community, as is a monastery.

Whenever there is patterned social interaction among people who have established a self-sufficiency—where interaction with outsiders is much less common than with insiders, and where the social organization itself fulfills the diverse needs of the individuals—then we say, "Here is a community." Communities normally have physical boundaries, but not always. So, for example, we sometimes describe American Jews as a community, or American blacks as a community. We mean by this that within the United States there exists interaction and social patterns among Jewish people which simultaneously unites them and to some extent sets them off from others in many areas of life. This is also what we mean by a black community.

Whether or not a given group is a community is often debatable, but to the extent that we can establish it as a self-sufficient social organization, we can so designate it.

Societies Are the Most Inclusive Form of Organization

The last form of social organization is society, and it is also the most difficult to describe and to understand since it is the most distant of all social organizations. We can define society simply as the *largest social organization whose patterns make a significant difference to the individual's actions. It is the social organization within which all other social organizations exist.* Within society we will find a host of dyads, groups, formal organizations, and communities, each affected in part by its location in society. Society is a social organization which has a long history, longer than any of its actors, and usually longer than other social organizations. It is embedded in its past; it is enduring.

Usually, sociologists go further and make society even more complex. Some, like Marion Levy (1952), point out that to be a society, an organization must have the characteristic that recruitment of new members comes through sexual reproduction, at least in part. The boundaries of societies are sometimes difficult to pinpoint. Are they defined by borders, by language, by religion, by history? In the modern world, society is usually the same thing as the nation-state (a political entity), but even here there are problems. Some nations, such as Cyprus or the U.S.S.R., are really two or more societies, with the nation being an artificial attempt to forge a new society by increasing interaction among the several societies and by establishing formal patterns for all to follow.

Some sociologists have developed an elaborate description of societies. Talcott Parsons and others describe societies as *systems of interrelated parts,* called structures or institutions. Societies develop parts in order to meet the requirements for survival. Society, therefore, is made up of political, economic, familial, religious, and military structures, each necessary for survival, each developed to meet the complex and diverse set of circumstances that confront it. The increased complexity of society described by some, however, should not keep us from recognizing the fact that society is like all other forms of social organization: It is made up of individuals who interact and develop social patterns.

The 1970s and 1980s have made most people aware of the fact that we live in a world order as well as in society. Sociologists are all too aware of this. People interact all over the world. Representatives of societies meet, interact through letters or the press, and make agreements. Economic matters are increasingly worldwide: The labor problems in the United States are in part caused by decisions made in corporations which know no societal boundaries. The prosperity of the farmer in the United States is linked to worldwide economic patterns. Perhaps it is no longer accurate to call society the "largest" social organization whose patterns are significant. It is all a matter of degree, however: Laws, rules, class structures, formal organizations, groups, and continuous interaction probably are still far more internal to each rather than among societies. Exceptions are real however, and increasingly important. To the extent that interaction and social patterns characterize the world, the world itself is a worldwide social order within which society must be understood.

SOCIAL ORGANIZATION SEEMS TO SIT RIGHT ON TOP OF US

Let us first summarize what we know about social organization: Humans act...sometimes without others in mind, sometimes with others in mind (*social action*). Sometimes others consider us as they act (*social interaction*). Sometimes interaction is brief, sometimes interaction goes on for a while and patterns are established (*patterned social interaction*). Patterned social interaction is also called *social organization;* social organization can be described as either (a) a dyad, (b) a group, (c) a formal organization, (d) a community, or (e) a society.

We are all part of a number of dyads and groups.

We are all part of a number of dyads and groups.

Usually, however, each of these is embedded in larger social organization, such as larger groups and formal organizations.

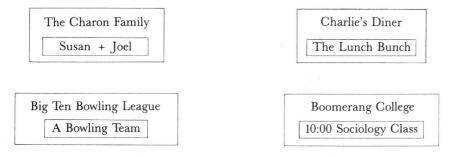

And these dyads, groups, and formal organizations are part of

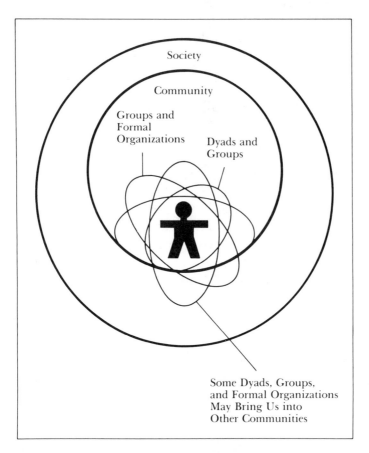

FIGURE 3–1   The Individual within Social Organization

communities, which are in turn located in society. The patterns that develop in each are influenced by the larger social organizations of which it is a part. Each one of us is in the middle of a large number of circles located within larger and larger circles (Figure 3–1).

Dyads and societies are alike: They have patterns established through people interacting over time. Humans are constantly developing and learning the various patterns. We are all located within a large number of social organizations, and the patterns of each affect what we do. Some sociologists will argue that we are prisoners in these patterns, that we take them for granted or do not even realize they are there, and that our social action becomes almost completely habitual because of the routines they impose. This is the argument put forth in the next few chapters as we look at the nature of these patterns. The argument will be made that these patterns are powerful forces, that they control and shape us, and that the individual has almost no freedom because of them. This kind of determinism in fact represents what many sociologists see. We see humans *caused* by social organization. If we are free, then our freedom can be understood only after considering the ways we are determined.

Many sociologists are not satisfied with determinism. They believe that humans act back, humans are more than pawns of social organization; society not only makes us, *we make society*. We must also understand how individuals choose, create their own social organization, rebel, act creatively, and control their own lives. The second view, which we might call an *active* view of the human being, will be discussed in Chapter 11.

QUESTIONS TO CONSIDER

1. What is the meaning of each of the following concepts? Can you give an example of each? Social action? Social interaction? Patterned social interaction? Dyads? Groups? Primary groups? Secondary groups? Formal organizations? Communities? Societies?
2. Are we in fact almost always social actors? Give some instances where people act without taking others into account.
3. Can you think of a situation in which you acted contrary to what you normally do because of others in the situation? Can you think of an instance in which interaction did in fact lead you down a path you never thought you would go? Is there an organization you belong to in which social patterns contradict your belief system?
4. What exactly is the view of the human being expressed in this chapter? Is it accurate?

RECOMMENDED READING

The following works discuss interaction and social groups:

ARONSON, ELLIOT. 1980. *The social animal.* 3d ed. San Francisco: W. H. Freeman.
CAPLOW, THEODORE. 1968. *Two against one.* Englewood Cliffs, N.J.: Prentice-Hall.
COOLEY, CHARLES H. 1909. *Social organization.* New York: Scribner's.
CROSBIE, PAUL V. 1975. *Interaction in small groups.* New York: Macmillan.

FESTINGER, LEON. 1956. *When prophecy fails*. Minneapolis: University of Minnesota Press.

FINE, GARY ALAN. 1979. Small groups and culture creation. *American Sociological Review* 44: 733–745.

GOFFMAN, ERVING. 1959. *The presentation of self in everyday life*. Garden City, N.Y.: Double-day/Anchor.

MCCALL, GEORGE, and J. L. SIMMONS. 1978. *Identities and interaction*. 2d ed. New York: Free Press.

MILLS, THEODORE M. 1967. *The sociology of small groups*. Englewood Cliffs, N.J.: Prentice-Hall.

SHILS, EDWARD S., and MORRIS JANOWITZ. 1948. Cohesion and disintegration in the Wehrmacht in World War II. *Public Opinion Quarterly* 12: 280–294.

SIMMEL, GEORG. [1908] 1950. The isolated individual and the dyad. In *The sociology of Georg Simmel*, ed. Kurt Wolff, 118–144. Glencoe, Ill.: Free Press.

THIBAUT, J. W., and H. H. KELLY. 1959. *The social psychology of groups*. New York: Wiley.

THRASHER, FREDERIC. 1927. *The gang*. Chicago: University of Chicago Press.

WARRINER, CHARLES K. 1956. Groups are real: An affirmation. *American Sociological Review* 21: 549–554.

WEBER, MAX. [1922] 1957. *Theory of social and economic organization*. Trans. A. M. Henderson and Talcott Parsons. New York: Free Press.

The following works are good discussions of formal organizations:

BLAU, PETER M., and WILLIAM R. SCOTT. 1962. *Formal organizations*. San Francisco: Chandler.

BUCKLEY, WILLIAM. 1967. *Sociology and modern systems theory*. Englewood Cliffs, N.J.: Prentice-Hall.

ETZIONI, AMITAI. 1961. *A Comparative analysis of complex organizations*. Glencoe, Ill.: Free Press.

GOULDNER, ALVIN. 1954. *Patterns of industrial bureaucracy*. New York: Free Press.

GROSS, EDWARD, and AMITAI ETZIONI. 1985. *Organizations in society*. Englewood Cliffs, N.J.: Prentice-Hall.

HALL, RICHARD. 1977. *Organizations, structure, and process*. 2d ed. Englewood Cliffs, N.J.: Prentice-Hall.

KANTER, ROSABETH. 1977. *Men and women of the corporation*. New York: Basic Books.

KANTER, ROSABETH, and B. A. STEIN, eds. 1979. *Life in organizations*. New York: Basic Books.

KATZ, DANIEL, and ROBERT KAHN. 1966. *The social psychology of organizations*. New York: Wiley.

MORGAN, GARETH. 1986. *Images of organization*. Beverly Hills, Calif.: Sage Publications.

OLSEN, MARVIN E. 1978. *The process of social organization*. New York: Holt, Rinehart & Winston.

PERROW, CHARLES. 1986. *Complex organizations: A critical essay*. 3d ed. New York: Random House.

PETERS, THOMAS J., and ROBERT H. WATERMAN, JR. 1982. *In search of excellence*. New York: Warner Books.

PRESTHUS, ROBERT. 1978. *The organizational society*. New York: St. Martin's Press.

SIMMEL, GEORG. [1902–1903] 1950. Metropolis and mental life. *The sociology of Georg Simmel*, ed. Kurt Wolff, 409–426. Glencoe, Ill.: Free Press.

WHYTE, WILLIAM H. 1956. *The organization man*. New York: Simon & Schuster.

The following works are good discussions of communities and societies:

DAVIS, KINGSLEY. 1949. *Human society*. New York: Macmillan.

ERIKSON, KAI T. 1977. *Everything in its path*. New York: Simon & Schuster.

FISCHER, CLAUDE. 1984. *The urban experience*. 2d ed. New York: Harcourt Brace Jovanovich.

FRISBY, DAVID, and DEREK SAYER. 1986. *Society.* New York: Tavistock, Ellis Horwood, and Methuen.

GANS, HERBERT J. 1982. *The urban villagers.* 2d ed. New York: Free Press.

GOFFMAN, ERVING. 1961. *Asylums.* Chicago: Aldine.

KANTER, ROSABETH. 1972. *Commitment and community.* Cambridge, Mass.: Harvard University Press.

LEVY, MARION J. 1952. *The structure of society.* Princeton, N.J.: Princeton University Press.

LIEBOW, ELLIOT. 1967. *Tally's corner.* Boston: Little, Brown.

PALEN, J. JOHN. 1981. *The urban world.* 2d ed. New York: McGraw-Hill.

WALLERSTEIN, IMMANUEL. 1974. *The modern world system.* New York: Academic Press.

WIRTH, LOUIS. 1938. Urbanism as a way of life. *American Journal of Sociology* 44: 3–24.

Youth Kneeling before a Prelate by Il Guercino (Giovanni Francesco
Barbieri) (1591–1666). Pen and brown ink. 23.5 x 19.1 cm. The
Metropolitan Museum of Art, New York. Rogers Fund, 1908.
(08.227.29). Reprinted with permission.

4

Social Structure

When humans act toward each other over time they develop patterns, and these patterns come to be more and more important to what they do when they are around each other. Instead of always having to figure out what other people are expecting, we come to know what others expect, and we act without thinking too much about our actions. Many times the individual learns the patterns already established before he or she comes onto the scene and acts without realizing so much has been determined by factors outside his or her control.

WE ALL FILL POSITIONS IN SOCIAL STRUCTURE

One of the patterns in social organization is called *social structure*. It refers to the fact that individuals in their acts toward each other are patterned in terms of their *position* in the interaction. Everyone has a "place" in interaction and people come to act toward each other according to their place. This occurs at all levels of organization—from dyads to societies. I know when we get together what you expect of me in my place, and I know what to expect of you in your place. If our positions are *friends* we know what to expect from each other: "Well, Marty, a real friend doesn't just rip into me but tries to help me work out my problem." We usually do not have the same expectations for each other: I may expect you to make more of the decisions, you may expect me to protect you from "toughies"; I may expect you to be the funny guy, you may expect me to be cool in the face of adversity. As friends we might expect each other to be loyal, to share beliefs, concerns, and problems, but even here my expectations of you will probably differ from your expectations of me because of the way the relationship develops. If you are female and I am male, this might affect the structure that develops between us.

In groups, formal organizations, communities, and societies, we may be assigned positions already developed for us, and when in those positions people will act toward us accordingly. We will do what is expected in our positions, and we will expect others to act "right" in their positions. Part of our socialization, part of learning within any social organization, is to learn our place or position and the relevant positions of others. My boss, my secretary, the janitor who cleans my office, my office partners, the planning people down the hall, the boss's son, the top advertising executive—all are positions I learn to relate to.

Often we want to learn these positions in order to know what to do around others and what to expect from the others with whom we interact, and also to know how much we can bend the rules and do some of our own thing. For example, both teacher and student learn their own and others' positions within the college. In relation to each other a teacher in a classroom may expect from the student good performance on an exam, a certain amount of respect, a seeking, questioning attitude (but only perhaps to a certain point), no cheating, agreement to abide by the rules set up by the teacher (or by the class). The teacher in turn is expected to prepare for class, to give fair exams and fair grades, and to talk at a level which the student understands. This only begins to describe the social structure that develops between teacher and students. We might also describe the similarities among the social structures that develop in all university classrooms, and we might isolate some unique things in each structure due to the interaction among actors. We might describe a general teacher position that students learn as a result of being in a few classrooms, as well as the particular position of each teacher. So while many structures are made up of positions the individual learns elsewhere, each structure is in some ways unique because each develops through particular interaction.

A social structure, then, *consists of the total number of positions within the social organization. Positions are interrelated, they form a network, and they cannot be described singly.* Thus, a teacher is described in relation to students, a husband in relation to wife, a boss in relation to employees, a colonel in relation to those under his or her command. There can be two positions as in a dyad or millions of positions as in a community or society.

A position is like a slot. This is an impersonal word, and suggests that people merely fill slots as they interact with others. But in a sense that is exactly what we do. As we interact with others we focus our perceptions and actions and expectations on *where we are in relation to others*—on their positions or slots in the social structure. The technical name for position is *status position*. (Some sociologists prefer the term *status* or *role,* but position or status position is more descriptive for our purposes here.)

ROLES ARE ATTACHED TO POSITIONS

People come to focus their expectations of behavior not on the person himself or herself but on the position of the person within the interaction. Sociologists use the term *norms* to refer to the expectations people have of one another. A norm can be informal and can be agreed upon by people in a dyad or group, or it can be formal, written down in a constitution, charter, or contract. A norm can be stated or it can be inferred from people's actions—from what people say and do. A norm can be violated and only meet with mild disapproval (you are foolish; I'm going to pretend I didn't see that; stop it!), or its violation might be met with fines, imprisonment, or even death.

Most of the time we are hardly aware of norms. They are implicit in situations, accepted by us but not something we think about consciously. We are expected to wear clothes in public, to be polite to people we meet, not to embarrass strangers, to drive on the right side of the street, to use utensils when we eat. These kinds of norms only become obvious to us when they are violated. Some norms, on the other hand, are very clear to us, explicit, very much a part of our conscious life. "I must succeed in college because my parents are paying for my education and they expect it." "I'd better be home by seven because Betty expects me to be prompt." We are also clear as to the penalties for violating them. "I'd better be prepared for class; my instructor expects it, and he will embarrass me if he calls on me and I'm not prepared." "I must produce at my job; my boss expects it, and if I am to be promoted I had better do what she expects."

Every status position within every social structure has a set of norms or expectations attached to it. This set of expectations is called a *role*. When someone "plays a role," he or she acts according to the expectations of others. We are actors on a stage—we have parts, which are status positions, and we act according to the direction of others, which is a role. So a social structure = a set of status positions; a role = a set of expectations or norms attached to a status position; and the actor enters a social structure, fills a status position, and learns the expectations or role, and acts—that is, meets the expectations, plays the role.

A family group is a good example for illustrating norms, roles, status positions, and social structure. Charlie has certain expectations (norms) for Alice that have developed between them over time. She is his wife (status position), and he expects her to have the primary responsibility for child rearing and for dealing with relatives. She is expected to listen to his gripes about his boss, to give him encouragement concerning his professional life, to be nice to his friends, to be patient with his impatience, and to spend the family funds carefully. Alice, on the other hand, expects Charlie, her husband (status position), to share in housework, to prepare the meals, to play with the children, to listen to her gripes about her boss, to encourage her to pursue her professional growth, and to know what to do in a weather emergency or when the plumbing breaks down. Each set of expectations between Alice and Charlie constitutes a role, and the role is located within a dyad. Yet the children are also part of the social organization (the family group) within which the dyad is located. Charlie must also conform to their expectations of him as father (a status position), such as putting them to bed, being kind, reading to them, taking them to the movies occasionally, bragging about them to others, punishing and rewarding them for certain kinds of behavior. Charlie fills two separate status positions—husband and father—and the role expectations between them may be partly the same, different but complementary, or may be in direct conflict.

Charlie's roles in the family are also defined by many people outside the family. His parents may have expectations such as be nice to your wife, do not spank your children, and be sure to bring your family to see us every Sunday afternoon. And Charlie's roles in the family are also defined by neighbors, friends, maybe his employer, the community, and the society. There are even written laws governing his roles (concerning physical abuse, for example, or neglect, or the education of his children). So each of Charlie's roles in the family is a cluster of norms, which comes from people within and outside the group.

So it is with the other social organizations of which Charlie is part: his office staff, his bowling team, his night school class, his church, his friendship group, and the dyad relationship he has with Maurice. Within each he plays a role—acts according to the expectations of others—defined by those within and outside the social structure.

ROLE CONFLICT OCCURS WHEN PEOPLE FACE CONFLICTING SETS OF EXPECTATIONS

Playing roles is not always easy for Charlie or for us. Roles bring problems. They are meant to make interaction easier by helping us know what to do. But in the real world we often do not know what to do because if we act according to one set of expectations we fail to meet another set that is important to us. We are faced with *role conflict*. There are several kinds of role conflict.

One Person Has Contradictory Expectations of Another (Intrasender Conflict)

Sometimes a person (or persons) expects us to do contradictory things in our role. ("My parents say they expect me to be independent, but they treat me like a child.") Katz and Kahn (1966) call this kind of role conflict *intrasender conflict*. The congregation of the First Lutheran Church expects its minister to be a moral leader, to take sides, to work for justice and equality, but at the same time it does not want him to get involved in migrant labor issues (since members of the congregation use migrant labor). I sometimes find myself expecting my children to keep their rooms spotlessly clean but have a lot of fun playing too—this surely can create role conflict for them! Students expect instructors to be personal, to show interest in them, to treat them as individuals, yet instructors must also grade everyone impersonally—otherwise they are charged with having "favorites." A young man might expect his lover to be popular with others yet loyal to him, sexually naive and sexually open, dependent and independent simultaneously, and smart around others, dumb around him.

Most of us are at some time or other in positions where the same people expect incompatible actions from us. Role conflict may or may not become serious. If it is serious, something must change—other people's expectations must change, or the individual must leave the relationship or a compromise must be worked out. At the very least, the individual must choose one kind of behavior and not let the conflict bother him or her. Probably one of the most important reasons we leave positions is that other people, perhaps without even realizing it, make demands on us that are so contradictory it is impossible for us to meet them.

Some People Have One Set of Expectations of a Person and Other People Have a Contradictory Set (Intersender Conflict)

An individual may be subject to contradictory expectations from different people. Daniel's dad expects him to fight back, and Daniel's mom expects him never to get into fights. Democratic Party leaders expect the president to choose a loyal party person; the public may demand an honest person; the feminists, a woman; and Chicanos, a Chicano. The president of the college might expect the vice president to "get rid of deadwood," the faculty might expect him or her to represent them in a favorable light to the president, and the faculty union might demand that the vice president do only what the union contract spells out.

A Person Plays Roles that Conflict with Each Other (Interrole Conflict)

There may be conflict between roles where one person is both, say, wife and professional, soldier and Christian, social scientist and social reformer, student and working person, political radical and corporate lawyer, or world peacemaker and defender of the nation's security. Some individuals who fill positions whose roles may seem to conflict may not feel conflict at all, since they may be able to isolate the roles so as not to see the relationship between them. In fact, most of the time we play one role at a time, not thinking of the other roles within our other social organizations. However, we become aware of conflict when the performing of one role must exclude performing the other—for example, when we put all our time in one, making it impossible to perform the other (I can't study because I have to work, or I'd like to come home for the weekend but my boyfriend wants me to help him study). When conflict reaches an unbearable point, we leave one of the roles. The conflict between the role of son to my mother and the role of husband to my wife may lead to unbearable conflict—and divorce. Or the professional man or woman, unable to meet the demands of being husband or wife, may also work to escape one of the roles. Escape may amount to deemphasizing or giving less attention to one role rather than leaving it entirely.

The Actor Does Not Fit the Role (Person-Role Conflict)

A role may be too demanding, or too difficult, or too boring, or too unethical, or too time-consuming. Each individual has expectations and abilities he or she brings to the role, and although the role shapes the person to a high degree, some people find certain roles to be unsuitable for them. Some of us simply refuse to fight in war, conform to the student position, or accept the role of husband. Some actors cannot take the pressures of criticism, some rich people the burden of wealth where other people suffer poverty, and some older people the low prestige which normally comes with retirement. We do not always have a choice, however. Many of us simply adjust to the positions we are in and make the best of it. Others leave.

WE NEGOTIATE ROLES AS WELL AS BEING SHAPED BY ROLES

The fact of role conflict suggests that playing roles is not done by sleep walkers but by human beings who must work out each role actively, at least to some extent; we choose what we do, we shape our roles. Some sociologists emphasize that playing a role is a matter of "negotiating," that roles are a result of not only other people's expectations, but also our own expectations. We all enter status positions, others define what we are supposed to do, we tell them through what we do how we define the role, and through interaction the roles are formed. Of course, too much creativity in defining roles may upset interaction, even to the point of our being expelled from the social organization, but some of it is inevitable, expected, and necessary for both the actor and the organization.

Although we are individuals who negotiate our roles with others, it would be a mistake to underestimate the power of role definition by others. The role is to some extent independent of us—the expectations are "out there," and we are shaped accordingly.

An excellent example of the power of role definition by others is a study done in California by Philip Zimbardo. Zimbardo (1972) tested what would happen to people if he isolated them from the outside world for a couple of weeks, and set up a situation in which some of them played the role of guards and some prisoners. We might guess that they had a good time, that they realized it was only a game, and that they did not come to their roles seriously. But this did not happen. Within a few days these people *became* their roles—the guards acted brutally, the prisoners really "wanted out." The situation actually became so nightmarish that the study had to be ended much earlier than planned. Remember, these were "mature, emotionally stable, normal, intelligent college students from middle-class homes throughout the United States and Canada....None had any criminal record...." Here is Zimbardo's description of what happened:

> At the end of only six days we had to close down our mock prison because what we saw was frightening. It was no longer apparent to most of the students (or to us) where reality ended and their roles began. The majority had indeed become prisoners or guards....There were dramatic changes in virtually every aspect of their behavior, thinking, and feeling....we saw some boys (guards) treat others as if they were despicable animals, taking pleasure in cruelty, while other boys (prisoners) become servile, dehumanized robots who thought only of escape, of their own individual survival, and of their mounting hatred for the guards. (p. 4)

STATUS POSITIONS FORM OUR IDENTITIES

Much of our socialization involves learning about the many status positions and roles in the world. The child learns how fire fighters and dentists work, learns what grocery clerks and teachers do. The child learns what mom and dad do, what bad guys do, and what good students do. The child plays at these roles, and in playing them displays a recognition that he or she knows the expectations attached to each.

We give names to status positions and this makes it easier for us when we meet other people. We learn what a *friend* is, and we are influenced by our learning when we decide to interact with someone as a friend. We also may learn the status position of wife, son, teacher, plumber, president, secretary, man, woman, minister, clerk, listener, quarterback, assistant, convicted criminal, boss, or movie producer. All nouns we call people by that imply relationships with others are names we give to status positions. These labels help us identify others; we know who others are if we can label them. When we meet someone at a party and learn the person's identifying labels in the larger world, we may call up images of the person according to his or her label or position—oh, you're a doctor (probably rich and smart); oh, you're a teacher (teachers are awfully stuffy). Of course, we are often in error in assigning personal qualities on the basis of position, but naming positions is one way we are able to know what to do in situations, it is one way to know what others expect of us, what to expect of them, and what to expect of ourselves.

One of the reasons this naming process is important is that it helps us know who we are. *The names we declare to other people and to ourselves are our "identities."* If you ask me who I am, I can tell you by naming my positions. I am a husband. A father. A professor. A sociologist. Al and Rose Charon's oldest son. A resident of Moorhead. An American citizen. All these make up my identities. (We might also declare that we are honest, or intelligent, or loving, or good looking, but we are only describing some of the qualities we associate with our positions.)

Peter Berger describes an individual who has just become a commissioned officer in the army. He plays the role, but at first he is distanced from it:

> [He] will at first be at least slightly embarrassed by the salutes he now receives from the enlisted men he meets on his way. Probably he will respond to them in a friendly, almost apologetic manner. The new insignia on his uniform are at that point still something that he has merely put on, almost like a disguise. Indeed, the new officer may even tell himself and

others that underneath he is still the same person, that he simply has new responsibilities....This attitude is not likely to last very long. In order to carry out his new role of officer, our man must maintain a certain bearing. (1963, 98)

The actor *becomes the role*. He takes on the identity:

With every salute given and accepted (along, of course, with a hundred other ceremonial acts that enhance his new status) our man is fortified in his new bearing....He not only acts like an officer, he feels like one. Gone are the embarrassment, the apologetic attitude, the I'm-just-another-guy-really grin. If on some occasion an enlisted man should fail to salute with the appropriate amount of enthusiasm or even commit the unthinkable act of failing to salute at all, our officer is not merely going to punish a violation of military regulations. He will be driven with every fiber of his being to redress an offense against the appointed order of his cosmos. (1963, 98)

Each of us is therefore many people, each one associated with a status position. We *become* our status positions, we think of ourselves in terms of those positions, and we announce these positions to others in how we act in the world. This is who I am! And as others know "who we are," they are influenced to act toward us accordingly.

We have, up to now, described two qualities that arise from our status positions. These are "role" and "identity," how we are expected to act and who we are. There is more to positions than this, however.

POSITIONS ARE UNEQUAL

It is probably obvious by now that status positions are not usually equal. Inequality seems to be inherent in all social structures, at least to some degree. Even in a dyad there is inequality as a rule, and this is certainly true of all groups, formal organizations, communities, and societies. As people interact, some always emerge with more of some things than the others. It was that way with Elaine and me. Our relationship started with me courting her, with me wanting her more than she wanted me, with her calling the shots and getting her way. It had to be that way at first: She had so many people in love with her and I was lonely. Gradually things shifted. She liked me! As she broke her friendships with others and became dependent on me, we became more and more equal, and we probably retained a delicate balance of equality for a short time. Eventually I became more powerful in the relationship. This may sound crude and it is oversimplified, but still that relationship, like all relationships, can be understood in terms of inequality, with some status positions more privileged and powerful than the others. If we try to diagram social structures, we end up organizing them in a hierarchy of higher/lower positions (Figure 4–1).

FIGURE 4–1   Status Positions within Three Social Structures

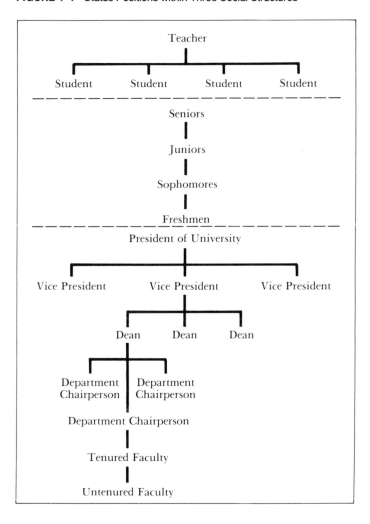

All social structures imply inequality—but what exactly is inequality? Sociologists usually describe three different qualities associated with position and causing inequality: power, prestige, and privilege. People in a social structure have various degrees of these qualities attached to their positions. A high position usually has more power associated with it than a lower position (a president is high in power, an enlisted person in the army has low power). "Power" means *the opportunity that one has for achieving his or her will in social organization.* Some positions give the holder opportunity to direct others and the organization according to his or her will. Some positions require that holders obey others. "Get elected to office, then make changes in the city council." "Get promoted and you won't have to take orders anymore—you'll give them." Indeed, many of us seek promotion in order to have more control over our own lives and to be more powerful within social organization.

In society, the positions of Supreme Court justice and U.S. president mean power. So too, do positions of cabinet officer, FBI director, and chiefs of staff. Certain members of Congress have high power, especially if they are positioned in key committees or in the political parties. Corporate executives are in especially key positions to determine the direction of society and various communities. Union officials and representatives of certain organizations such as the American Medical Association and the American Bar Association are very influential. Imagine society as made up of thousands of positions, some far more powerful than others. If a person achieves one of these positions, then he or she has the power that goes with it.

Indeed, as we shall emphasize in future chapters, *class* should be regarded as a position in society, as should *gender* and *race*. In most societies—certainly our own—people are positioned according to these criteria too. Such positions are assigned to us at birth. Each one gives the individual more or less power in relation to others.

Most social organizations have status positions which differ in the amount of *prestige* associated with them. Being a senior at college probably has little power, but it does carry a certain amount of prestige. Certainly few would prefer to be a freshman. "Prestige" refers to *the honor that people accord the position.* We defer to others according to their position; we often ignore those who are in lower positions than our own. If you become a Supreme Court justice in the United States, you are honored because of the position you fill. If you are rich or president of a corporation or a medical doctor, many people will be attracted to you because of your position. And many of us seek the honor associated with high positions.

In most societies men have more prestige than women, and in almost all societies being upper class brings more prestige than poverty. One is honored or dishonored for race and religion too. All of these are positions in society's social structure.

Prestige can change over time. If Americans no longer respect the police or the president or Supreme Court justices, it means those positions have declined in prestige. It is often easier to list positions which do not carry great prestige: private in the army, prostitute, freshman, the "baby" of the family, the nontenured instructor on a college faculty. Prestige is subjective. If most of us do not regard a certain position as having high prestige, that does not mean all of us agree; nor does it necessarily mean that people who fill it cannot be quite good at it or gain a great deal of satisfaction (or money) from doing it. But prestige cannot be ignored. It is real. In every social organization prestige is one of the qualities associated with all positions.

Finally, positions also bring with them certain *privileges,* the good things, so to speak, that come to the person filling the status position. These may be high income and other material benefits, opportunity to choose one's own office furniture, choice of home, long vacations, a secretary, free schooling, a classy car. Even dyads and groups have privileges associated with positions: being able to call on other people's assistance, knowledge, skills, or loyalty, people to share problems with, people who bring us excitement or entertainment or love.

Nothing seems more obvious than all the privileges which go with class position in society. Not only comfort, but health, good education, opportunities for children, and increased choices in every aspect of life go with high class position, whereas hardship, lack of economic and educational opportunity, and poor health go with low class position. Being male or female, black, red, or white also makes significant differences in privileges.

Besides role and identity, then, each status position also has a certain amount of power, a certain degree of prestige, and some privileges attached. Power, prestige, and privileges create inequality within the social structure. Usually—but not always—these three qualities will be interrelated: For example, the greater one's power, the higher will be the prestige and the more privileges one will receive. Privilege and prestige will normally bring greater power, and privilege will bring prestige, prestige privilege.

OUR POSITIONS ALSO GIVE US OUR PERSPECTIVES

Not only do our positions within social structure provide us with our roles, our power, our prestige, our privileges, and our identities, but they also determine our perspectives—they give us the eyeglasses through which we look at the world. People define the world according to where they are located. A boss and an employee may both value the business (an organization) but for different reasons. Each will have a different perspective on it (and perhaps also on American business in general). Teachers and students see school differently (after all, teachers gain their livelihood from their positions; students may see their position as a hurdle to overcome). Rich people and poor people differ in their outlooks or perspectives, and seniors and freshmen are far from the same in how they view the university.

Our status position also may influence how we look at the world in general. Not only does a corporate executive see the corporation differently from the man or woman who works on the assembly line, but the executive probably has a different view of government, American capitalism, foreign policy, American education, and perhaps even religion. What we think is true, what we value, what we believe is wrong or right in the world arises from our position.

Why should this be true? First of all, we are socialized into our positions: not only in how to act but also how to think, how to approach understanding reality. Teachers interact and share a view of their profession, the school, students, and American education. Principals socialize teachers how to look at reality, as do teachers' colleges, and even students.

The second reason that positions give rise to perspectives is that each position should be thought of as a location in organization, an angle, a point from which one views the world. Each position is a different angle, each will cause people to see reality from that angle. In truth, the president of the United States must see foreign policy differently from the rest of us. If nothing more, he or she knows that his or her decisions will have lasting influence. Rich and poor, men and women, boss and employee, quarterback and running back: Each must necessarily see the world from a different perspective.

This is a very simple point. However, it is very profound, and should tell us all something about human differences.

SUMMARY: THE IMPORTANCE OF STRUCTURE

We can now see how important social structure is to what we do. People are actors who fill positions in social structure (either developed through interaction or already defined), and these positions have norms (roles) attached telling them what to do and what not to do in the positions. We can refuse to conform, but if we do we will either be punished, lose the position, or upset the interaction we probably want to be a part of. We learn to label others according to their positions and we come to have expectations of them. We also label ourselves; we become our status positions; who we are and who we announce to others we are—our identities—arise from our status positions. Also, we find that in each of our positions there are normally people below us or higher than us; we are located in a system that grants each position some power, some prestige, and some privileges. If we want to change our lot, we may try hard to change our position. We know that other positions mean more power, privilege, or prestige. And, finally, our eyeglasses on the world—our perspectives—are anchored in our positions. What we do in life, what we get from it, who we are, and what we think depend on the positions we fill.

Figure 4–2 summarizes what we have discussed in Chapters 3 and 4 about social organization and social structure. In Chapter 5 we will shift our attention to *society* and its social structures, perhaps the most important structures of all.

QUESTIONS TO CONSIDER

1. What is the meaning of "social structure"?
2. What is the meaning of: power, privilege, prestige, role, identity, perspective, and status position?

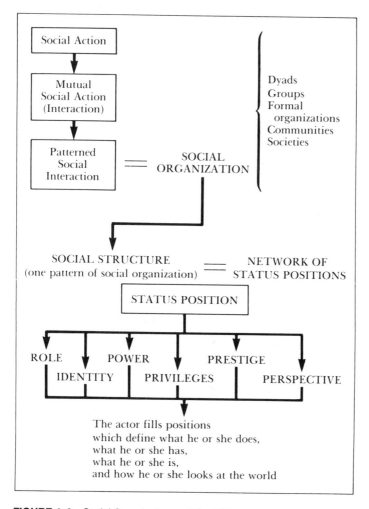

FIGURE 4–2 Social Organization and Social Structure

3. Describe the meaning of role conflict. Give some examples of role conflict.

4. What exactly is the description of the human being presented in this chapter? Is it accurate? Is it appealing? Is it useful?

5. Why is social structure a necessary aspect of all social organization? What is its importance for the individual?

6. Hey! Who are you anyway? What are your identities? Are they in fact status positions you fill in social organization?

RECOMMENDED READING

The following works are good introductions to the meaning and importance of social structure:

BERGER, PETER L. 1963. *Invitation to sociology.* Garden City, N.Y.: Doubleday.

BLAU, PETER M. 1955. *The dynamics of bureaucracy.* Chicago: University of Chicago Press.

BLAU, PETER M. 1964. *Exchange and power in social life.* New York: Wiley.

BLAU, PETER M. 1971. *Bureaucracy in modern society.* 2d ed. New York: Random House.

BLAU, PETER M. 1975. *Approaches to the study of social structure.* New York: Free Press.

BUCKLEY, WALTER. 1967. *Sociology and modern systems theory.* Englewood Cliffs, N.J.: Prentice-Hall.

CAPLOW, THEODORE. 1968. *Two against one.* Englewood Cliffs, N.J.: Prentice-Hall.

DURKHEIM, EMILE. [1893] 1964. *The division of labor in society.* Trans. George Simpson. New York: Free Press.

EMERSON, RICHARD. 1962. Power-dependence relations. *American Sociological Review* 27: 31–41.

ETZIONI, AMITAI. 1964. *Modern organizations.* Englewood Cliffs, N.J.: Prentice-Hall.

GAMSON, WILLIAM A. 1968. *Power and discontent.* Homewood, Ill.: Dorsey.

GOULDNER, ALVIN. 1954. *Patterns of industrial bureaucracy.* New York: Free Press.

HALL, RICHARD H. 1977. *Organizations, structures and process.* Englewood Cliffs, N.J.: Prentice-Hall.

KANTER, ROSABETH. 1977. *Men and women of the corporation.* New York: Basic Books.

KATZ, DANIEL, ROBERT L. KAHN. 1966. *The social psychology of organizations.* New York: Wiley.

LIEBOW, ELLIOTT. 1967. *Tally's corner.* Boston: Little, Brown.

LIPSET, SEYMOUR M., MARTIN TROW, and JAMES COLEMAN. 1956. *Union democracy.* New York: Free Press.

MERTON, ROBERT K. 1968. *Social theory and social structure.* New York: Free Press.

MICHELS, ROBERT. [1915] 1962. *Political parties.* Trans. Eden and Cedar Paul. New York: Free Press.

MILGRAM, STANLEY. 1963. Behavioral study of obedience. *Journal of Abnormal and Social Psychology* 67: 371–378.

MILGRAM, STANLEY. 1973. *Obedience to authority: An experimental view.* New York: Harper & Row.

MILLS, THEODORE M. 1967. *The sociology of small groups.* Englewood Cliffs, N.J.: Prentice-Hall.

OLSEN, MARVIN E. 1978. *The process of social organization.* New York: Holt, Rinehart & Winston.

PERROW, CHARLES. 1986. *Complex organizations: A critical essay.* 3d ed. New York: Random House.

PRESTHUS, ROBERT. 1978. *The organizational society.* New York: St. Martin's Press.

RUSSELL, BERTRAND. 1938. *Power.* New York: Norton.

WEBER, MAX. [1922] 1968. *Economy and society.* Trans. Ephraim Fischoff, et al. New York: Bedminster Press.

WEBER, MAX. 1946. *From Max Weber: Essays in sociology.* Eds. and trans. H. H. Gerth and C. Wright Mills. New York: Oxford University Press.

WHYTE, WILLIAM F. 1949. The social structure of the restaurant. *American Sociological Review* 54: 302–310.

WRONG, DENNIS. 1980. *Power, its forms, bases and uses.* New York: Harper & Row.

ZIMBARDO, PHILIP. 1972. Pathology of imprisonment. *Society* 9: 4–8.

Miner's Wives (1948) by Ben Shahn (1898–1969). Egg tempera
on board. 48 x 36 inches. Philadelphia Museum of Art. Given
by Wright S. Ludington. Reprinted with permission.

5

Inequality in Society

It is part of the American way of thinking that this is a land of opportunity for all—that all have a roughly equal chance to succeed. It is difficult for us to see that inequality is built into the very nature of society, that we are in fact all part of social structures that work against equal opportunity. Most of us spend much of our lives trying to "make it" in a society that we perceive to be open.

Yet, we have always had inequality in society. We have always had a few privileged people and a large number of poor. We have always had class inheritance within families, and we have always had opportunities limited by class in virtually every aspect of life: government, education, health care, choice of neighborhood, and the law and the courts, to name a few.

There are several reasons why this is difficult for us to see. First, equal opportunity has been a central part of the heritage we have been taught. Second, many people have come here from societies with much less opportunity, and have been able to succeed here where they would not have had the opportunity to succeed in their homelands. Third, because of the tremendous industrial growth in the United States throughout most of this century, almost everyone's position has improved over their parents'. Finally, inequality is easily hidden, especially at the extremes of poverty and wealth.

Inequality in both income and wealth has characterized the

TABLE 5–1   Share of Income Received by Each Fifth of Families, 1983 (in percent)

LOWEST FIFTH	SECOND FIFTH	MIDDLE FIFTH	FOURTH FIFTH	HIGHEST FIFTH	TOP 5 PERCENT
4.7	11.1	17.1	24.4	42.7	15.8

Source: U.S. Bureau of the Census, *Current Population Reports* Series P-60, No. 140.

United States since its beginnings. To begin to appreciate its existence, consider Table 5-1, which describes family income in 1983. The top fifth earned 43 percent; the bottom three-fifths earned 34 percent. The top 5 percent earned the same as the bottom 40 percent! This inequality has not changed very much since 1947 (see Table 5-2).

These figures describe the inequality in *yearly income.* An even better assessment of inequality is the total wealth of U.S. families—property, savings, investments, business assets, and so on. It is much more difficult to get reliable data on wealth. We know that in 1962 about 20 percent of American families owned 76 percent of the total wealth; the bottom 20 percent of families owned less than 1 percent of the wealth; and 60 percent owned 8 ½ percent of the wealth (Figure 5–1).

Michael Harrington described a similar picture in 1972:

> The bottom quarter of the society has no wealth at all—or, more accurately, has negative wealth since many of its members are net debtors. The next 55.9 percent of the people have 23.8 percent of the wealth. Adding those two groups together, the cumulative figure shows that 81.3 percent of the Americans hold 23.8 percent of the wealth. In short, four-fifths of the people own somewhat less than the top 0.5 percent. Moreover, the wealth of the "ordinary" (nonrich) citizen takes the form of homes (which are, as has just been noted, heavily mortgaged), automobiles (purchased on credit) and other consumers' durables, like washing machines and television sets. In

TABLE 5–2   Income Distribution Since 1947 (in percent)

	LOWEST FIFTH	SECOND FIFTH	MIDDLE FIFTH	FOURTH FIFTH	HIGHEST FIFTH	TOP 5 PERCENT
1983	4.7	11.1	17.1	24.4	42.7	15.8
1973	5.5	11.9	17.5	24.0	41.1	15.5
1963	5.0	12.1	17.7	24.0	41.2	15.8
1953	4.7	12.5	18.0	23.9	40.9	15.7
1947	5.1	11.8	16.7	23.2	43.3	17.5

Source: U.S. Bureau of the Census, *Current Population Reports,* Series P-60, No. 140.

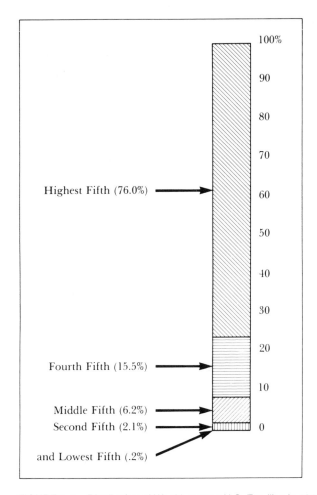

100%

90

80

70

Highest Fifth (76.0%) ⟶ 60

50

40

30

20

Fourth Fifth (15.5%) ⟶

10

Middle Fifth (6.2%) ⟶
Second Fifth (2.1%) ⟶ 0

and Lowest Fifth (.2%) ⟶

FIGURE 5–1 Distribution of Wealth among U.S. Families in 1962 (*Source:* U.S. Office of Management and Budget, Executive Office of the President, 1973.)

other words, most of the "wealth" of four-fifths of the population does not itself generate income or wealth. (1980, p. 155)

In 1983, data was compiled for the Federal Reserve (U.S. Congress, 1986). Some examples of its findings are:

1. The top 10 percent owns 90 percent of the stock in the United States. (The top 1 percent owns 60 percent.)
2. The top 10 percent owns 73 percent of the total wealth. (The top 1 percent owns 42 percent.)
3. Between 1963 and 1983 the top 0.5 percent went up in its average wealth by

147 percent. The next 9.5 percent went up by about 65 percent, the bottom 90 percent by 45 percent.

Although details sometimes vary, the general picture that emerges is consistent and clear:

1.   Income and wealth are highly concentrated in the United States, and taxes have not significantly altered that concentration.

2.   The inequality that exists today is highly consistent with the inequality which has existed at least since the Civil War.

3.   Although there is opportunity to change one's position in the system of inequality, most of that change is due to the fact that everyone is moving up due to economic opportunity. *Relative position* does not change easily, and when it does, it is usually slightly above or below one's parents.

4.   Beginning in the 1970s, the occupational system has changed considerably from what it was—fewer jobs in industry, more service jobs, less opportunity in various professions—causing less opportunity for upward mobility than characterized this society from its beginning. For the first time in this society's history, children are faced with the prospect of accepting a lower position in the class structure than the position held by their parents.

THE MEANING OF SOCIAL CLASS

One's "class" is most easily understood as one's *position in the class structure in society*. One's "position" depends on economic criteria, the two most easily understood being income and wealth. Any class structure has many positions or ranks. Sociologists differ as to the number of classes in the United States, some dividing everyone into two classes and others distinguishing as many as twelve. Where one draws a line and declares "Here is a class!" depends on what one wants to understand. For example, Daniel Rossides (1976) identifies five: upper, upper-middle, lower-middle, working, and lower. Michael Harrington, on the other hand, is interested in three: the poor, the nonrich, and the rich. Some sociologists examine class as occupational levels: business executives, professionals, managers, white-collar workers, blue-collar workers, and unskilled workers, for example.

No matter how it is defined, class has rich meaning in sociology. It is similar to all other positions in social organization. The higher one's class, for example, the more *power* one has. Having high rank means that one is able to influence the economic and political order more regularly than those who hold low rank or live in poverty. When economic resources matter in interaction with others, the higher one's class, the greater the probability of achieving one's will. Research since the 1950s has documented how much power those who sit at the top of United States corporations have, from determining futures of whole communities to influencing American foreign policy. At the other end of the spectrum, one thing we know about the poor in all societies is that they are powerless to control their economic destiny, they are dependent on others for survival, and they have almost no impact on the direction of the economic and political order.

Class also brings *prestige*—or lack of it. High position brings admittance to the "right" clubs and neighborhoods, the admiration of others, public recognition. It brings the opportunity to buy goods that symbolize importance (expensive cars, diamonds, designer dresses, large homes). Low position in the class structure elicits contempt from many, dishonor from some, and sympathy from still others. Low class position in society is not usually sought, except by those few individuals who do not care about such matters. In a society where class is so important, competition for class position "sets up a contest for dignity," a struggle to win over others in order to gain "self respect" (Sennett and Cobb 1972,147–148).

Of course, class position influences the *privileges* one has in life, or what Max Weber called "life chances" or opportunities. Class influences educational opportunities, life expectancy, health, occupational placement, marital satisfaction, nutrition, level of economic hardship, and occupational and geographical mobility. Class influences all of these matters for our children, and it influences the quality of life we will have after we retire. Class also influences whether or not a person is arrested for a crime and, once arrested, the likelihood of being denied bail, going to trial, being found guilty, and getting a heavy sentence.

Class position also brings *role expectations*. We tend to marry those in approximately the same class position as we are in. Poverty brings lower educational expectations than being in the upper class does. Indeed, whether or not one goes to college, which college one goes to, what one's major is, and whether or not one goes on to graduate school is influenced by expectations of family and friends that are largely class based. How one is supposed to act around others, how one is supposed to speak, what one is supposed to like in food, drink, and music are also tied to class. Weber described such expectations as the *"lifestyle"* associated with class position.

Class position also tells the individual who he or she is. It is one of our central *identities*. Others label us by class, we think of ourselves in terms of class, and through our actions and dress we announce our class to others. Like all of our identities, class identity makes a difference in how we act around others.

Class position helps determine our *perspective* and the actions that arise from perspective. For example, if we are upper class we tend to believe in the political system and we are more likely to be active politically. We are also much more likely to be conservative on economic matters. We are more interested in how to save money rather than how to pay our bills. Class influences what we think about gender roles, religion, education, and child-rearing practices.

The class structure, therefore, is like all other structures of which we are a part: It is made up of status positions (classes), each one of which influences the actor's actions by giving him or her power, prestige, privilege, identity, role, and perspective.

GENDER AND RACE

In our society—and in most—race and gender act in the same way as class. We are born boys or girls, and this places us in a social position, with role, identity, power, privilege, prestige, and perspective attached. For a long time the position of women in society had a particular set of expectations attached. Men expected women to be housewives and mothers (roles), and many women assumed these as their identities. This, combined with other factors, brought women a lower position in relation to men with less power in home and society, fewer privileges (in educational, sexual, and economic choices, for example), and lower prestige (traditionally the woman's prestige was tied to her husband's). Of course, many people no longer accept this gender structure without question. Both men and women are beginning to see that gender differentiation into positions as well as the ranking that comes with it is, after all, a *social structure,* a social pattern that has emerged over many years. Biology does not command it, and thus, like all else human, it remains the same or it changes as people interact over time. Such patterns, embedded in history, are difficult to alter overnight. Although it is clear that thinking about male and female differences has changed, it is also clear that in the 1980s one's gender is still important for a host of matters, from occupational and political opportunities to even role expectations and identity for many.

We also fill positions in society based on race. A racial structure has always characterized the United States: Those who came here from Europe conquered the Native-American, enslaved the black, and eventually used the Asian and Mexican as cheap labor. In each case a social structure developed in which nonwhite status remained low. Segregation was written into the law, and segregation between races was embedded in neighborhood patterns. Role expectations, power, prestige, privileges, identity, and perspective arose from such positions. Like the gender structure, the racial structure has had a long time to develop and is very difficult to change. We might change our ideas about what is just, but it is far more difficult to assure greater opportunities for racial minorities. Where significant change is tried—such as affirmative action or busing students to achieve more equal education—cries of outrage and distress are heard from many quarters. Many whites—like many men and many in the upper classes—do not welcome losing their favored position in society.

CLASS, RACE, AND GENDER STRUCTURES ARE SPECIAL SOCIAL STRUCTURES

Class, race, and gender, then, are all social structures in society, but they are also very special structures, characterized by the following qualities:

1. *The individual is placed in all three at birth.* One's initial position depends on biology or family.

2. *The individual's position in all three is perpetuated by the family.* That is, the family directly places the individual (for example, by determining race or bestowing wealth), and the family teaches the position to the individual (for example, how to act "like a man" or how to be a "young lady" or the way that "people like us" are supposed to act).

3. *The individual's position in these structures influences placement in most other structures.* In government, in business, in the military, or in education, what one can achieve is influenced by class, race, and gender positions.

4. *The individual's position in these structures is generally fixed.* We cannot, of course, change race or gender. Class position may be less fixed, but for the vast majority of people class placement at birth has a strong influence: The rich

generally stay rich, the poor stay poor, and those in between move slightly above or below where they were born. Class position at birth acts as a constraining force: It does not determine where one ends up, but it acts as an important influence.

5. *Various institutions in society cooperate to protect and perpetuate the structures as they have developed.* Political, legal, economic, educational, religious, and kinship institutions socialize us, encourage us, and reward us to accept the existing social patterns and our place in them. Often, the structures are presented as just, moral, and natural; opposition to them is condemned as immoral or unpatriotic and is subject to punishment.

6. *These structures are embedded in a long history.* They are therefore difficult to challenge and/or alter. We are used to them. They are less open to challenge than structures created in other forms of organization such as groups and formal organizations. It is difficult for most of us to see realistic alternatives to them, for they seem so much an integral part of our taken-for-granted world. And, even for those of us who wish to do away with them or at least to alter them, it is often difficult to make sound suggestions as to how to institute workable changes.

The term *social stratification* or *stratification system* is generally applied to *social structures that are relatively fixed, such as class, race, and gender.* Stratification, of course, is a concept borrowed from geology, where it refers to the layering of rocks beneath the earth's surface. A system of *social stratification* is similar to layers of rock: It is ageless, relatively permanent, and individuals in each layer are embedded. Yet, of course, earthquakes sometimes occur—relatively rare but powerful—and foundations are shaken and profound change occurs.

SOCIAL STRATIFICATION AFFECTS PLACEMENT IN OTHER SOCIAL ORGANIZATIONS

Social stratification is evidenced in everyday interaction. It is woven through concrete situations in our lives as well as in the organizations we join. For example, whatever the woman's position is in society affects her position in the family. If women are expected to be housewives and mothers in society, and if they are excluded from full participation in the occupational system, then we can expect that John will be influenced to treat Mary, his wife, this way, as well as Betty, his daughter. This will affect his actions toward them, the opportunities he provides them, and the privileges he is willing to grant. As society changes, however, as women enter in force into the occupational order, and as they rise in it, Mary will be encouraged to gain more power for herself in relation to John, privileges will be more negotiable, and John will be influenced to change how he acts.

As blacks pulled together in the 1950s and 1960s, they changed their relative position in society to some extent. Then their positions were improved in communities, in businesses, in groups, and in schools. So long as our social stratification system based on race stays intact in American society, however, it will continue to have an effect on opportunities for individual blacks in all social organizations.

Class, race, and gender affect placement of the individual in every social organization. An interesting study by Rosabeth Kanter (1977) examines how sexual stratification affects relationships in formal organizations. First of all, the jobs people hold are influenced by their sex, women holding almost none of the supervisory and managerial jobs and almost all of the clerical jobs, which "have low status, little autonomy or opportunity for growth, and generally low pay." The image of men as rational, efficient, and objective and the stereotype of women as emotional, irrational, and concerned with helping others have worked to exclude and to justify the exclusion of women from the centers of power and responsibility. Management has been defined as "masculine," more routine office jobs as "feminine." The corporation therefore has masculine and feminine status positions, and the sex stratification in society carries over into the corporation. Indeed, Kanter also points out that women gain their job satisfaction, rewards, and prestige through the men they are dependent on. They judge themselves and each other in terms of who (the man) they work for and not the skills they exhibit and tasks they perform.

Kanter also underlines the emphasis that managers place on social similarity in their circle of power, hiring and promoting people on the basis of "who fits in," who they can "trust," who is "their own kind." The result is that men develop a closed world, promoting and hiring other *men*. As Kanter says, "Men reproduce themselves in their own image." This, of course, excludes most women from the status positions of power. Managers in the corporation that Kanter observed felt "uncomfortable having to communicate with women" they saw as not sharing "masculine" social qualities. Women, unlike men, were also seen as lacking the loyalty necessary to the organization (since they also have loyalties to family). Finally, Kanter points out that even if women are promoted to high positions, they encounter the burden of overcoming the stereotype of the "woman boss" that both men and women have come to share. In short, women in the corporation are placed according to the stratification system that has developed throughout society.

THE ORIGIN OF SOCIAL STRATIFICATION SYSTEMS

No one really knows exactly how or why stratification systems have developed in almost every known society. We can argue, of course, as we did in Chapter 4, that social structure is simply an inevitable pattern and that one characteristic of social structures is that they are almost always unequal. Sociologists have tried to better understand the dynamics involved in the rise of stratification systems. Usually the explanation revolves around the interplay of conflict and power.

If we define conflict as *the struggle over whatever happens to be valued among people,* then we can understand that whenever something is valued that cannot belong to everyone equally there will be conflict. Some win; some lose. Those who win consolidate their position as well as they can; those who lose are in a poorer position to win in the future. The power of those who win increases over time, and the social patterns that emerge in society tend to favor their interests. Gerhard Lenski (1966, Chapter 3) most clearly describes this process:

1. In any society, whatever is valued will always be in short supply. When this occurs, humans will pursue these values for themselves, and some, because of personal or group advantage, will be more successful than others in obtaining them.

2. Obtaining and keeping material goods through the successful application of personal or group power brings an accumulation of goods (privileges). Both power and privileges in turn bring prestige.

3. Both prestige and control over valued goods bring, in turn, more power. The circle is complete (Figure 5–2).

4. The system of distribution, created out of personal power, is eventually justified; it becomes "legitimated," regarded as right. Inequality is protected by the power of a few, and eventually by the ideas developed in society.

5. Finally, advantages are passed down to offspring. Possession of goods is not associated with person but with family. A class system is thus created and perpetuated.

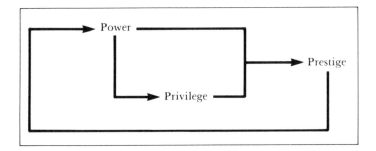

FIGURE 5–2 The Interplay of Power, Privilege, and Prestige: The Origin of Stratification

Lenski's description is obviously aimed at the class system. However, similar arguments have been applied to the origin of both racial and gender stratification. In the case of race, whites dominated blacks, Native-Americans, Asian-Americans, and Mexican-Americans; took land or cheap labor from these groups; and then set up a society that systematically excluded these groups from full participation. There was conflict among groups with unequal power, and a social structure developed that has been perpetuated throughout American life.

Inequality between men and women goes back even further. We can imagine that men won in relation to women where there was conflict; they accumulated power and established a system of perpetuated inequality. Winning might have been based on physical strength or just the fact that women were at a disadvantage because of continuous pregnancy, but men emerged at the top of society, women at the bottom.

Whatever its origin, however, social stratification is real, and its effects are the same as any social structure. New members are assigned positions, and those positions have important consequences for the lives of those members.

SOCIAL MOBILITY

Social mobility refers to *change in the individual's class either in relation to his or her parents or during his or her own lifetime.* We say that a society has high mobility where individuals are likely to change their positions.

We cannot change gender or race. These are called *ascribed* qualities (rather than *achieved*) and cannot be escaped. Individual blacks or women can achieve much in society in spite of the fact that it is more difficult for them, but they will always remain black or women. As long as these qualities are important for placing people in society, the individual will be affected.

Class is slightly different. Because it is based on economic criteria, it is *achieved,* at least to some degree. Societies differ in the extent to which class mobility is possible. Realistically, however, there is not very much movement for the vast majority of people in the class system. In the United States as well as other Western industrialized societies, inherited wealth, family socialization, and family contacts (or lack of them) place real limits on mobility. To rise out of the depths of poverty and acquire wealth is not possible except for the very few, and to lose family fortune and upper-class position is highly unlikely except for the very reckless. Working- and middle-class children are generally satisfied with improving their position over their parents, but few have realistic expectations of making it into the ranks of the upper class. Poverty imprisons people, and it is difficult for those caught up in it to do much more than survive. There is no question that people can move up in the class system in America, but movement is very limited. It also seems to be true that opportunity is no greater in the United States than it is in other industrialized nations.

One of the reasons it seems that there is a great deal of mobility in the United States is that we have experienced high prosperity and rapid economic change for so long. This has meant that almost all people have been able to improve their positions relative to their parents', and over their own lifetimes people have been able to improve their positions relative to where they began. Yet, this has not meant that there has been great opportunity for the individual to improve his or her position relative to others in the class structure. Movement up the social structure is predictably small.

STRUCTURAL CHANGE

Nothing stays the same. Over time structures change, and as they do opportunities open up for people long deprived, and those who have always had privileges are forced to give some up. For example, since World War II there has been a steady change in the relationship between men and women. As women have entered the paid labor force, expectations have changed as to what women's roles are, and their power, privileges, and prestige have all become more equal in relation to men. Widespread use of birth control, the women's movement, longer lifespans, and increasing independence of children have all contributed to this changing gender structure.

The racial structure has also changed. Migration of blacks to urban centers and to the North since 1900 has increased their power in relation to whites, and this has been accompanied by both privileges and prestige. Although it is a mistake to believe that the United States has achieved anything approaching racial equality, there have been many improvements since 1900. Organization and protest, legislation, executive action, and Supreme Court decisions, as well as achievements by individual blacks, have all worked to alter the social structure.

Change in the class structure is more difficult and complex. The relative numbers, power, privilege, and prestige of the upper class has remained fairly stable since the Civil War, perhaps fluctuating in short periods. The number of those in the poverty class has probably declined since the Civil War, yet since World War II this class has also remained stable. This class was and is a powerless class without prestige, and although its privileges have risen, they have not risen nearly to the extent that they have for other classes.

When we define class in terms of *occupation*, then the class structure has changed considerably. In 1900, farm workers constituted 37.6 percent of the population; in 1979 they were 2.8 percent. In the same period those in white-collar occupations went from 17.6 percent to 50.9 percent.

The whole nature of work and the occupations necessary for the work force have dramatically changed, but it is not clear that the class structure (measured in income or wealth) has changed very much. It is probably accurate to maintain that the jobs of the working class, the jobs of the middle class, and the type of wealth that the upper class controls have all changed, as has the relative size of the classes (larger middle, smaller working class). Change is not great, however, when we examine relative wealth, income, power, prestige, and privilege in the United States.

MARX'S VIEW OF SOCIAL STRATIFICATION

Karl Marx (1848), more than any other, emphasized the central importance of social stratification or social structure to our lives. Most sociologists do not accept all of Marx's perspective, but like Durkheim's *Suicide,* his writings have spurred research, debate, and new directions of analysis.

Marx believed that *economic class* was central to society since all other systems of inequality were dependent on it. Within economic class there were basically two possible positions for each person—owner or worker. Marx understood that ownership of the means of production (the land or the factories or the slaves depending on the historical period of society) confers many benefits, especially power in relation to others. No resource is more important to the individual than control over property that produces the valued goods of the society, since that means control over people's jobs as well as all the things they need for survival. That position, he argued, also makes it possible to control all other institutions in society, such as the police, the courts, the army, the government, religion, and the educational system. People who had the land or factories or slaves could thus control people's lives directly through jobs and goods produced and indirectly through controlling the various institutional systems of society. The workers, on the other hand, were powerless, lacking the resources (at least until they decided to unite and overthrow the owners) to raise their position in relation to the propertied class. Indeed, Marx argued, the workers would become more and more poor, less and less powerful.

Marx also argued that the powerful determined the *ideas* that prevailed in the society. They were in the best position to teach what they considered the truth, and the ideas they taught would be in their interests—for example, competition is a law of nature, poverty is inevitable, protection of private property is more important than protection of workers' rights or people's lives. With the army, police, government, law, religion, and ideas as tools, the wealthy propertied have the tools to perpetuate a system from which they gain many privileges.

Marx saw that those who have the power also have the privileges in the society. They have longer lives, better health care, better educational opportunities, more leisure time, comfort, and security. The workers, he believed, are doomed to poverty. Their dependent position places them at the mercy of the propertied; they are exploited, used as tools, and granted only those privileges that will keep them dependent.

Marx predicted an eventual end to the class structure in society and its replacement by a structure of equality. Because class position is so important in determining how people act, Marx believed that real social change can come only when the old class structure is destroyed. Marx did not believe that it is possible to reform the class structure through laws or education, since in the long run such reforms only serve to protect the powerful. Eventually, however, the workers will become conscious of their exploited position and realize that they can do something to change society. They will organize, overthrow the existing social structure, and create a society of equality.

Although Marx has many critics, among sociologists as well as others, in a way this testifies to his importance. For Marx's ideas, like those of the other classical sociologists, have been the focus of many important debates in sociology and have encouraged a great deal of theoretical and empirical work. Marx long ago saw what many of us understand all too well today. Our *position* in the economic order is central to determining much of who we are, what we do, and what we think. It is central to our power and privilege in society. And this social structure, built over many generations and centuries, is very stable. Few share Marx's belief that it will eventually be overthrown and replaced with a nonstratified society, although many people take the spirit of Marx and try to work for a less stratified society. The insights of Marx as well as the continuing experience of sociology tell us that the stratification systems, around for a long time, accepted as right by most, defended in a number of subtle ways by those who gain from them, perpetuated through the family, are highly resistant to change.

SUMMARY

Humans are located in society by class, race, and gender. The individual's location, or position, brings role, identity, perspective, power, privilege, and prestige.

Class, race, and gender are part of special social structures called *social stratification systems*. The individual's position within such structures arises from birth and family. Position is impossible or difficult to change, and the structures change slowly.

Social stratification systems arise out of conflict and power, and they are protected by society's institutions and the ideas that most of society's people learn to believe.

Social structure in society is one of the most central concepts in all of sociology. Sociologists have long documented the lack of privileges among the poor, the power of the wealthy, the role expectations and lack of privileges that constrain women, and the lack of privileges and power of racial minorities. This research has established the continuing importance of position in America's social structures.

Social structure arises in all interaction over time, and it is part of every social organization, from dyads to societies. Our status positions not only include class, race, and gender—discussed in this chapter—but also student, oldest son, friend, clerk, and mayor—discussed in Chapter 4.

Besides social structure, there is another pattern that emerges when people interact over time. That pattern is *culture,* and it is the topic of the next chapter. Before turning to that, however, take a moment to examine Figure 5–3, which integrates social action, interaction, patterned social interaction (social organization), social structure, and culture.

QUESTIONS TO CONSIDER

1. What is the meaning of class? What is the meaning of social stratification? What is the meaning of social mobility?
2. If class, race, and gender are positions within social structures, then we should be able to describe them in terms of power, prestige, privileges, role, identity, and perspective. Can you do this?
3. Social structures change. Perhaps we are witnessing very profound changes in society's social structure based on gender. What evidence do you have that this structure is actually changing?
4. One hundred years from now, will there be inequality in this society based on class? On race? On gender? Why is it so difficult to change these systems of inequality?
5. Evaluate social mobility in your own family. To what extent have your parents improved on the relative class position of your grandparents? To what extent has your relative class position improved over your

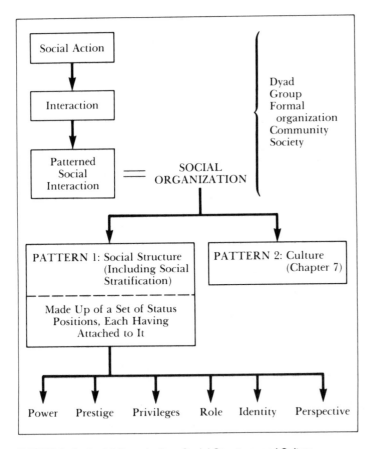

FIGURE 5–3   Social Organization, Social Structure, and Culture

parents? So what if our generation cannot do better than our own
parents—does it really matter?

RECOMMENDED READING

The following works are excellent introductions to the study of social
class:

ABRAHAMSON, MARK, EPHRAIM H. MIZRUCHI, and CARLTON A. HORNUNG. 1976. *Stratification
    and mobility.* New York: Macmillan.
BEEGHLEY, LEONARD. 1983. *Living poorly in America.* New York: Praeger.
BEEGHLEY, LEONARD. 1989. *The structure of social stratification in the United States.* Boston:
    Allyn and Bacon.
BENDIX, REINHARD, and SEYMOUR MARTIN LIPSET. 1966. *Class, status and power.* New York:
    Free Press.

BLAU, PETER, and OTIS DUDLEY DUNCAN. 1967. *The American occupational structure.* New York: Wiley.

BLUMBERG, PAUL. 1980. *Inequality in an age of decline.* New York: Oxford University Press.

BOTTOMORE, TOM. 1964. *Elites in society.* New York: Basic Books.

BOTTOMORE, TOM. 1965. *Classes in modern society.* New York: Pantheon.

DAHRENDORF, RALF. 1959. *Class and class conflict in industrial society.* Stanford, Calif.: Stanford University Press.

DOMHOFF, G. WILLIAM. 1967. *Who rules America?* Englewood Cliffs, N.J.: Prentice-Hall.

EWEN, STUART. 1976. *Captains of consciousness.* New York: McGraw-Hill.

GILBERT, DENNIS, and JOSEPH A. KAHL. 1987. *The American class structure.* 3d ed. Chicago: The Dorsey Press.

HARRINGTON, MICHAEL. 1963. *The other America.* Baltimore: Penguin Books.

HARRINGTON, MICHAEL. 1980. *Decade of decision.* New York: Simon & Schuster.

HAWLEY, WILLIS. 1968. *The search for community power.* Englewood Cliffs, N.J.: Prentice-Hall.

HUNTER, FLOYD. 1953. *Community power structure.* Chapel Hill, N.C.: University of North Carolina Press.

KELLER, SUZANNE. 1963. *Beyond the ruling class: Strategic elites in modern society.* New York: Random House.

KERBO, HAROLD R. 1983. *Social stratification and inequality.* New York: McGraw-Hill.

KOLKO, GABRIEL. 1962. *Wealth and power in America.* New York: Praeger.

LENSKI, GERHARD. 1966. *Power and privilege: A theory of social stratification.* New York: McGraw-Hill.

LUNDBERG, FERDINAND. 1968. *Rich and super-rich.* Secaucus, N.J.: Lyle Stuart.

MARX, KARL. [1848] 1963. *The communist manifesto.* Trans. Eden Paul and Cedar Paul. New York: Russell & Russell.

MARX, KARL. 1964. *Selected writings in sociology and social philosophy.* eds. T. Bottomore and M. Rubel. Baltimore, Md.: Penguin.

MATRAS, JUDAH. 1984. *Social inequality.* 2nd ed. Englewood Cliffs, N.J.: Prentice-Hall.

MILLS, C. WRIGHT. 1956. *The power elite.* New York: Oxford University Press.

OLSEN, MARVIN E. 1978. *The process of social organization.* New York: Holt, Rinehart & Winston.

RAINWATER, LEE. 1974. *What money buys: Inequality and the social meanings of income.* New York: Basic Books.

ROSSIDES, DANIEL W. 1976. *The American class system: An introduction to social stratification.* Boston: Houghton Mifflin.

RYAN, WILLIAM. 1972. *Blaming the victim.* New York: Vantage.

SENNETT, RICHARD, and JONATHAN COBB. 1972. *The hidden injuries of class.* New York: Random House.

TUMIN, MELVIN M. 1967. *Social stratification: The forms and functions of inequality.* Englewood Cliffs, N.J.: Prentice-Hall.

TURKEL, STUDS. [1972] 1975. *Working.* New York: Avon Books.

U.S. CONGRESS. 1986. The Concentration of Wealth in the U.S. Washington, D.C.: Joint Economic Committee.

USEEM, MICHAEL. 1984. *The inner circle.* New York: Oxford University Press.

ZEITLIN, MAURICE. 1978. Who owns America? The same old gang. *The Progressive* 42: 14–19.

The following works are good introductions to dominant-minority relations (race, ethnic groups, and women):

BLALOCK, HUBERT M. 1979. *Black-white relations in the 1980s.* New York: Praeger.

BLAU, FRANCINE D. 1984. Women in the labor force: An overview. *Women: A feminist perspective,* 3d ed., ed. Jo Freeman, 297–315. Palo Alto: Mayfield.

BLAUNER, ROBERT. 1972. *Racial oppression in America.* New York: Harper & Row.

CARMICHAEL, STOKELY, and CHARLES HAMILTON. 1967. *Black power: The politics of liberation in America.* New York: Random House.

FARLEY, JOHN E. 1982. *Majority-minority relations.* Englewood Cliffs, N.J.: Prentice-Hall.

FREEMAN, JO, ed. 1984. *Women: A feminist perspective.* 3d ed. Palo Alto: Mayfield.

HOCHSCHILD, JENNIFER. 1984. *The new American dilemma.* New Haven, Conn.: Yale University Press.

JACOB, JOHN E. 1985. *The state of black America.* National Urban League.

KANTER, ROSABETH. 1977. *Men and women of the corporation.* New York: Basic Books.

LIEBOW, ELLIOT. 1967. *Tally's corner.* Boston: Little, Brown.

MYRDAL, GUNNAR. 1962. *An American dilemma.* New York: Harper & Row.

REID, JOHN. 1982. Black America in the 1980s. *Population Bulletin* 37 (4).

RIX, SARA (ed.). 1987–88. *The American woman.* New York: Norton.

SIMPSON, GEORGE EATON, and J. MILTON YINGER. 1972. *Racial and cultural minorities: An analysis of prejudice and discrimination.* 4th ed. New York: Harper & Row.

STOCKARD, JEAN, and MIRIAM M. JOHNSON. 1980. *Sex roles: Sex inequality and sex role development.* Englewood Cliffs, N.J.: Prentice-Hall.

TAVRIS, C., and C. WADE. 1984. *The longest war.* 2d ed. San Diego: Harcourt Brace Jovanovich.

U.S. COMMISSION ON CIVIL DISORDERS. 1968. *Report.* New York: The New York Times Co., Bantam Books.

VAN DEN BERGHE, PIERRE. 1967. *Race and racism: A comparative perspective.* New York: Wiley.

WAITE, LINDA. 1981. *U.S. women at work.* Washington, D.C.: Population Reference Bureau.

WEITZMAN, LENORE J. 1985. *The divorce revolution.* New York: Free Press.

WILSON, WILLIAM J. 1978. *The declining significance of race.* Chicago: The University of Chicago Press.

WILSON, WILLIAM. 1973. *Power, racism, and privilege.* New York: Macmillan.

WILSON, WILLIAM J. 1987. *The truly disadvantaged.* Chicago: University of Chicago Press.

X, MALCOLM, and ALEX HALEY. 1964. *The autobiography of Malcolm X.* New York: Grove Press.

YETMAN, NORMAN R., and C. HOY STEELE, eds. 1982. *Majority and minority: The dynamics of racial and ethnic relations.* 3d ed. Boston: Allyn & Bacon.

Snap the Whip (1873) by Winslow Homer (1836–1910), United States.
Cooper-Hewitt Museum, Smithsonian Institution/Art Resource, New
York. Gift of John Goldsmith Phillips, Jr.. (1947–4–60). Reprinted
with permission.

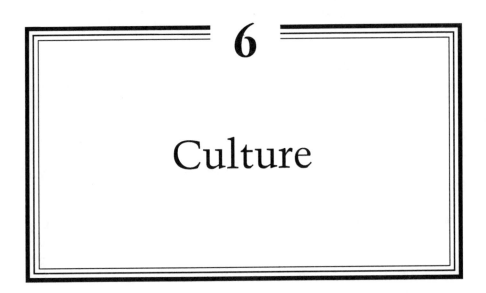

6

Culture

Culture is the second pattern of social organization. Like social structure it is developed in interaction over time; it determines much of what the individual does; and it allows for continuity, stability, and predictability among people.

CULTURE IS A SHARED PERSPECTIVE
OF THE WORLD

In the language of social science, *culture* does not mean violins, poetry, or art. *Culture is a perspective of the world that people come to share as they interact.* It is what people come to agree on, their consensus, their shared reality, their common ideas. The United States is a society whose people share a culture. And within the United States, each community, each formal organization, each group and dyad has its own culture (or what some social scientists call a *subculture,* since it is a culture *within* another culture). Whereas structure emphasizes differences (people relate to each other in terms of their different positions), culture emphasizes similarities (how we agree).

To be part of the "youth culture" in the United States, for example, is to share with a number of people certain ideas about truth, politics, authority, happiness, freedom, and music. On the street, in print and speech, on college campuses, concerts, and movies, a perspective develops as people share experiences and become increasingly similar to each other on the one hand, while becoming increasingly different from those outside their interaction. A common language develops among those who share the culture, reinforcing solidarity and excluding outsiders.

When Marsha and Henry interact they form their own unique culture too, in a sense. They talk things out and come to share views about each other, parents, adults, children, China, life, work, and the future. They say things to each other which only they fully understand since they have a common context within which to place those things. While others are straightfaced, they break out laughing at the same situation, funny only to them because they see it in a similar light.

Culture is what people come to share in their heads—their ideas about what is true, right, and important. These ideas guide us, they determine many of our choices, they have consequences beyond our heads. *Our culture, shared in interaction, constitutes our agreed-upon perspective of the world and directs our acts in the world.*

Culture Is Learned

Our ideas about the world are learned from each other through interaction in families, schools, and all forms of human social organization. Our ideas are anchored in our group life. We seek group support for what we believe; we test our ideas out with each other; we accept ideas that are supported by those people with whom we interact and who are important to us. We learn our culture and do not seriously think there are other ways of looking at the world. We are born into families and the culture shared there becomes central to our way of thinking. When we enter social organizations such as a school, a gang, a sorority, or a corporation, we come to learn the "right way to think," and if we wish to belong we come to believe in these cultures we learn. Belief is encouraged by the fact that social organizations are important to our identity, to our meaning as individuals. The ideas shared in social organization penetrate us; they become part of our heads and basic to our acts.

Culture distinguishes us from those with whom we do not interact. Isolation of a group, society, or other social organization means a unique view of the world; integration with others means less and less uniqueness.

Culture Is a Social Inheritance

Many social organizations we enter have existed for a long time; people who have power within them teach us their long-established "truths" so that we may become good members and the social organization will continue. Culture is a social inheritance; it consists of ideas that may have developed long before we were born. Our society, for example, has a history reaching beyond any individual's life, the ideas developed over time are taught to each generation and "truth" is anchored in interaction by people long dead. Examples of this are everywhere: Successful people must get a college diploma; women should get married and have children; romantic love should be the basis for marriage; making money is the best way to encourage people to work. Each child is taught this culture by the family, school, and church—those social organizations that are its carriers. We are socialized to accept the ideas of those in the positions of "knowing better," those who have many years of history on their side, a long tradition, rightness or God or science or whatever. Formal organizations have a history too, and so do communities and groups. We may contribute our ideas, but we are always confronted by a powerful force, a culture, that developed before we entered the scene and that we have little choice but to accept if we wish to continue interacting in the social organization.

Witness the individual who tries to break away from the culture. To break out of the culture is to stand alone, to chance being thrust from the social organization, or in some societies to be penalized with imprisonment or death. To reject the organization's definition of truth is to reject the organization itself—and one must be prepared either to be isolated or to join other organizations which share the "right" views, which turn out to have, of course, another culture.

We may change social organizations and therefore trade one culture for another. But each organization has a way of defining the world, a way of thinking, a set of rules, that it encourages its members to share, and we will be expected to join in too. We may adopt a radical perspective at college, then off we go to teach high school or to join in a business after graduation, and our beliefs change as we are cut off more and more from the people with whom we interacted at college. Some of us may leave our community or even our society to enter a new one. Over time the old culture will be gradually replaced with new ideas and rules. But this is difficult for most of us. We hesitate breaking off from one set of truths and having to learn a new way, a new culture.

A culture, then, is a shared perspective, a set of ideas that people develop and learn in interaction. These can be divided into (1) ideas about what is true, (2) ideas about what is worthwhile (values and goals), and (3) ideas concerning the correct way of doing things (norms). Let us examine each in turn.

CULTURE IS A BODY OF "TRUTH"

A culture is, first of all, a set of ideas concerning what is true or real. All people do not agree on what is true in the world. Each social organization develops a special world view that it holds to and teaches its members. Each society develops a culture that has a body of truths, and so will each community within society, each formal organization, group, and dyad. We share truths as we interact, and people with whom we do not interact have truths we cannot learn, understand, or believe. In Fargo, North Dakota, we believe that farming is the backbone of the United States, in Chicago we believe that farmers make too much money, and in Texas, that farming is big business. In the United States we believe that the Soviet Union is responsible for world conflict, while most Soviet citizens probably hold us responsible, and many in the developing nations see conflict arising because of both the Soviets and the Americans. Sociologists share their own truths, as do students at the University of Chicago, and to some extent, students all over the United States. A group may share beliefs about the nature of God, life, society; this is part of its culture. Baptists may hold that life is a testing ground for an afterlife existence, humanists may hold that the purpose of life is to seek goodness, and the National Association of Manufacturers may emphasize gaining powerful positions and increasing wealth. An automobile company's truth may be that the automobile is the mode of transportation that gives us the greatest independence, while an ecology group's truth may be that the automobile is responsible for poisoning us through air pollution.

Almost all of us like to think that our ideas about the world are true. Some of them probably are, but most of them we have come to accept not because of careful evidence, but because of our interaction. If we are honest with ourselves, we will realize that our ideas, by and large, are *cultural,* that they are formed in social organization and taught to us as members of organization. Even if they are to some extent true, they are also limited in capturing reality, since each is a focus, exaggerating certain aspects of reality, and ignoring other aspects. Can anyone truly believe he or she would have the same set of truths if born in the Soviet Union or Switzerland or Mexico or Japan? Can psychology majors truly believe that their truths would be the same if they had majored in sociology and interacted with sociologists? Can New Yorkers truly believe that their ideas about living would be the same if they had grown up in Great Falls, Montana, or Dallas, Texas?

We all have different ideas about the world, about what is and is not true. Those of us who are very careful are probably going to capture some ideas close to the truth. Most of us, however, will accept those ideas our organizations teach; our interaction is going to influence what we believe. If we understand this, then our disagreements with others will seem more like differences arising in interaction—cultural—than truth against falsehood. My good friend Larry is a neuropsychologist. When he and I discuss human beings we disagree a lot about why humans act as they do. He focuses on the brain; I focus on our social life; neither of us focuses on early childhood training. That is because each of us has accepted a culture associated with our profession, different from each other, and different from other social scientists. Of course we are going to disagree. Maybe he is in error; maybe I am; maybe we both are (how good is our evidence?). It is probably true, however, that we both have something important to say, and that our disagreement is largely cultural.

There are good reasons why a given society develops one set of truths rather than another. People develop a philosophy, a belief system, a view of reality that is *useful* to them. It works for their organization. We tend to believe ideas that successfully guide us in our action, that help us make sense out of the experiences that confront us, that support the organization. Social organizations develop truths over time as people work out ways of dealing with their environment. Truths are developed to solve the problems we face, to justify our actions, to justify the structures we create. In the end, ideas that work for a people's situation become their truths; and since every social organization is in a different situation and every social organization has a different history, cultures will be different.

"America is the land of opportunity. It is a just system. It is a place where all people can make it to the top. It is based on fair competition, which brings out the best qualities of the human being. If someone makes it in this system, he or she should be able to keep what he or she makes. If one does not make it, then chances are that person did not try hard enough." These ideas are cultural. They work well in the 1980s to protect the economic system and the social inequality that we have. They may or may not be true. Truth or falsehood depends on the evidence rather than on the fact that a majority believes these ideas.

It is far from this simple, however. Although on the one hand a people's particular body of truth may be functional for them, we must also remember the role of social structure in creating ideas. Power is an important aspect in all social structures; those who have the most power will have the most impact on creating the culture, and usually the ideas that prevail in social organization as part of its culture are ideas that most benefit those in power. It is not that they necessarily lie and mislead others; it is that their truths, highly consistent with their position in society, tend to prevail as *the* truths.

CULTURE IS A SET OF VALUES

Culture is also made up of ideas about what is worth working for (ends). These are of two kinds: values and goals. Sometimes the distinction between values and goals is difficult to make since both consist of ideas about what we should pursue, what purpose our action should have.

A *value* is *a long-range commitment of the organization or individual. It is a strong preference, an organizing principle around which goals are established and action takes place. A goal* is *a short-range objective in a specific situation by an individual or social organization.*

In most situations our choice of action depends on our value commitments. Is honesty or a college degree a more important value to us? Is God or school, friendship or family, materialism or love, freedom or equality, courage or safety, doing right or doing what is popular, the future, present, or past, people or things, getting a good education or getting a good job? We are guided by such values, and they in turn are developed in interaction with others.

All of us have several values we believe in. Often situations arise in which we must choose among values since if we follow one we cannot follow the others. Most of us, for example, value freedom, equality, and life, but when we are faced with a real situation to work out, some of these become more important to us than the others. An individual may favor equality for all people, but may also desire a certain job which he or she is afraid will be given to a minority candidate, and must then commit himself or herself either to equality or personal security. A person may value both a college education and an active social life, but that may also involve a choice on various occasions. Classes sometimes force us to choose between open-mindedness and the security that comes with certainty. Values are not simple guides, because they are often contradictory. Even so, if we examine ourselves closely, we will see a core of values that influence us in many situations.

We learn our values in interaction. Groups, formal organizations, communities, and society direct our priorities by teaching us a set of values. Every social organization has slightly different values, and we change as we change organization. The values society teaches us are difficult to question, since they normally seem like the only sensible ones. Organizations have a stake in teaching us to value certain things. If we become strongly committed to an organization, then its values become our own. If we spend all of our time interacting within an organization (for example, a certain community), then its values tend to become our own. Alternative values are difficult to accept if they do not have some social basis, that is, if they do not arise from an organization of which we feel a part. Strong value commitments normally reflect strong social commitments: to a religion, to a fraternity, to feminists, to a family, or to a political party, for example.

Strong commitments to a social organization means that the organization itself becomes an important value to the individual. We may be willing to give up time or money or even life for it; we may find our whole purpose in life tied to it. People sacrifice for families, they work hard for businesses; they volunteer for churches and charities; and they endanger their own lives for country. Sometimes it is because of what the social organization stands for; often it is because the organization itself has become a value.

Whatever values are developed in an organization will be largely functional for the organization. Like ideas about truth, values serve a purpose; they mobilize the individuals around desired ends and cause them to act in ways that aid the organization. It is no accident that corporations value profit and growth, the work ethic and capitalism, planning and noninterference by government. These values serve the corporation's stability and continuity, and employees are encouraged to acquire these as their personal values. Also, values, like truths, are most likely to reflect the values taught by and beneficial to those at the top of the social structure.

Values Are Reflected in Action

Our values are not necessarily what we choose on a questionnaire or what we say we believe in to our children or to our friends. Our stated values may only be what we are supposed to believe in. Values are really reflected in what we do, not what we say. It is our goals, decisions, and actions that reveal our values. I may tell others I value education, but others can see by my lack of interest in school that I do not. I may tell others I believe in love, but others can see that love is not reflected in my actions. The emphasis in this society on buying things, making lots of money, judging each other on the basis of wealth, reflects a value commitment to materialism by large numbers of people. Family life is less important today than it once was—no matter what we *say,* our decisions reflect the fact that other values have become more important to us.

The relationship between values and action is more complex than this. It may be that we act differently from what we say we believe in. Yet, what we say still can have a long-range impact. It is probably better to say "I believe in democracy" than to say "I believe in white supremacy," no matter what the reality of our action is. For if we say (and think) that we believe in democracy, someone can point out how our action contradicts our value, and there is some chance for us to alter our acts and bring them in line with our stated values. Equality, for example, is a value that Americans often espouse, but clearly have not followed in relation to racial minorities and women. The success of movements to alter society depends in part on their appeal to the value of equality. "If you really believe in equality, then show me through your acts that you are willing to do something to alter the unjust racial and gender stratification systems!" It would be much harder to appeal to those who espouse the natural superiority of whites and men and who say they value a society built on inequality.

There Is an American Value System, but It Is Complex and Often Inconsistent

The United States as a society has a value system which we have come to share over a long history. It is made up in part of the values of individualism, equality, and material success. Yet the argument can be made that we also value conformity, a segregated society, and material security. Listing American values is a difficult task because there are so many exceptions and contradictions. I realized this when I first read the well-known study by Robin Williams (1970) which attempted to isolate and analyze the American value system. The values that Williams listed—success, materialism, work, progress, practicality, democracy—seemed to conflict with other values many Americans hold, such as leisure, tradition, even racial supremacy.

Yet on a very general level Americans do share a value system, especially when we look at the United States in contrast to other societies like England or Kenya or China. In China, for example, cooperation, progress for society as a whole, and the importance of the family (no matter what political leaders say or do) are dominant. Individualism and personal happiness are emerging as very dominant values in the United States, and at the moment, other, more traditional values—sacrifice for family, hard work, duty to job and company—are becoming less important.

Within the United States each community also has a value system, influenced by the larger society but also unique because of the interaction that takes place in a particular community over time. Harlem, Minneapolis, Atlanta, Peoria, Harvard, Salt Lake City, and San Antonio are all communities in the United States. Each shares the dominant culture, yet each is somewhat unique in values emphasized. Some will have high commitment to family, some to work, some to religion, some to "law and order," some to radical change. Each formal organization also develops a value system, as does each group and each dyad.

As complex and contradictory as an organization's value system may be, it is still different from other organizations, and it is still important to what people do. Although individualism is not held by all Americans as the most important value, it seems to be an extremely important value to most from the very beginning of society. It weaves itself throughout our history, and, in the 1980s its place has become very prominent. It is an individualism bonded to materialism, and it is an individualism that sometimes includes free thinking, and sometimes not. It is an individualism which has all kinds of implications for our view of taxes, business, crime, athletics, and sex; it is an individualism which competes with values such as family, equality, responsibility to the poor and disadvantaged, and even a commitment to a liberal arts education.

CULTURE IS A SET OF GOALS

Goals, like values, make up the ends people work for. Goals are practical ends; values are moral ends. Goals are ends to be achieved and then replaced by other goals; values are general guides for action. Goals are the specific ends we organize our action around, the ends which create the problems we try to solve. Humans are problem solvers. Individually we establish goals to achieve, and we organize our efforts to achieve them; together in organizations we share goals to achieve and we cooperate to overcome the problems that may arise. A team cooperates to win a game or achieve first place. A corporation may try to increase profits 5 percent the first quarter of the year. A society may try to work out a peace treaty, lower inflation, or redistribute income through higher taxes for some. These are all goals.

Values are important for goals. They are our abstract long-range commitments which act to oversee our goals. We work for those goals which are consistent with our value commitments. My goals Sunday might include going to church in the morning, working for the United Fund in the afternoon, and spending time Sunday evening discussing religious issues with my children, all of which are consistent with my value commitment to religion. I also have longer-range goals consistent with this value: to become head of our church, to make the church a more meaningful experience for the congregation, to teach my children the value of religion. A person whose value is education might have the goals of graduating high school, graduating college, getting a graduate degree, teaching, encouraging his or her children to learn, and so on.

Values and goals are two components of culture. Like ideas about truth, they arise among people as interaction takes place over time. They are important for keeping the organization together, for transforming the individual into a cooperating actor, in a sense changing individual values and goals to organizational ones. Some sociologists emphasize the importance of common goals and values for the continuation of all organization. It is obviously difficult for cooperation to take place over time if there is not at least some agreement among the actors as to what should be worked for.

Culture means agreement, and individuals whose truths, values, and goals are contrary to those of the organizations in which they interact make it difficult for the organizations to succeed. Think of the dyad relationships with parent, friend, teacher, or employer. Without some agreement on ideas about reality, values, and goals, these dyads will experience conflict, tension, and perhaps dissolution.

CULTURE IS A SET OF NORMS

The set of norms we share is the fourth component of culture. We have earlier described norms as *the expectations we have for each other*—how we are supposed to act—the rules, the laws, the right way. Norms are associated with one's position and are thus part of structure (remember, they make up a *role*), but they are also associated with membership in the group, irrespective of position (they make up the *culture*).

In interaction, we come to agree on the rules of the game (the means used to achieve the ends), and we agree to operate within them while in the social organization. They may be simple procedures to be followed, or informal expectations, or traditions, laws, or morals. We each obey the norms for different reasons—moral commitment, fear, expectation of reward, or simply because we believe rules are necessary—but most of us do obey them. In fact, most of us never really think about it. We simply accept most of the norms we learn in organization since we are part of the organization. Often, we do not consider that alternative norms might be more rational.

Organizations need rules to function. A social organization can work only if members agree, at least to some extent, to give up personal beliefs about how people should act and accept the organization's beliefs. This need not involve moral agreement and usually does not, but each organization expects that certain procedures, laws, and traditions be followed. The extent to which rules are necessary is a subject for debate, but most of us would probably agree that some norms are necessary for all social organization. We expect each other to be on time, to help each other, to be faithful, to seek each other's company. The gang requires that new members go through initiation rites, demands personal bravery and loyalty to the gang above all other organizations, influences individuals to act cool, and asks everyone to contribute time and money to the group and to take orders from the leader. The bank expects employees to be honest, friendly to all customers, and cheerful; it sets up elaborate procedures to follow in order to guarantee accuracy and security; and it develops a set of criteria for promotion of employees. Communities and societies have customs and laws that all are expected to follow.

Every situation we enter is governed by norms. Eating, dressing, walking, driving, and even sleeping are governed by rules that have arisen over a long social history. The way we worship God, celebrate birth, mourn death, and even feel pain depends on society's norms. The range is almost endless: from simple procedures necessary for the functioning of an office to taboos whose violation is dealt with through execution.

Organization is built on the acceptance of norms to a great extent. We predict the actions of strangers on the street, on planes, and in stores. We expect that people will wait their turn, treat each other with respect, and act peaceably. One effect of violent random crime and hijacking is the undermining of long-accepted norms, leading to distrust and fear of others in situations once characterized by taken-for-granted trust.

These norms, then, exist in all social organization and are part of the pattern called culture. They influence or shape or control (depending on the situation) the individual's action. Some rules (such as laws) are obeyed because we realize that if we do not we will be punished or the society will be threatened; some rules, on the other hand, take on a moral significance, become our ideas of right and wrong; they become more than just rules, since conscience and guilt play a strong part in enforcement. Most social organizations will attempt to make their rules seem morally right. Sometimes they are successful; sometimes they are not. For some individuals a rule becomes a moral guide; for others a rule remains just a rule.

CULTURE, SUBCULTURE, AND COUNTER-CULTURE

Many sociologists reserve the term *culture* for the shared perspective of people in a whole *society* and then introduce other terms to refer to cultures within that society. They sometimes distinguish *subcultures, countercultures, group cultures,* and *dominant culture.* Subcultures are part of any distinctive community or group in society. Adolescents are sometimes described as forming a subculture, and so are various ethnic groups, such as black people or Jewish people. Subculture does *not* mean that the community has an "inferior" culture. No sociologist uses the term to mean that. The prefix "sub" should be taken to mean "within," not "inferior to."

The concept of *subculture* is an important one, for it reminds us that although there may be "an American culture," there are many highly distinctive groups and communities within America. At the same time, however, the term also implies that the subculture does not develop in a vacuum, that it is influenced by the larger culture in many complex and subtle ways. So, as Marvin Olsen points out, the juvenile gang that believes that it is right to steal cars may appear to be very different from the dominant culture, yet it, too, emphasizes monetary success and peer acceptance, and to that extent has been influenced by the dominant culture's values (1978,162–163).

The term *counterculture* is used to describe certain other cultures within the dominant societal culture. The counterculture, unlike the subculture, explicitly "rejects the norms and values which unite the dominant culture while the [subculture] finds ways of affirming the national culture and the fundamental value orientation of the dominant society" (Roberts, 1978, 114). The counterculture rejects the "central values of the culture, and a greater discrepancy exists *between* the culture and the counter-culture than *within* either one of them" (115).

Like every society, America has had important countercultures. The Bohemians of the 1920s, the Beatniks of the 1950s, and the Hippies of the 1960s are the most important examples. In each case communities separated themselves from the larger society and pursued radically different values, while offering certain people a real alternative to the dominant culture. These countercultures acted as an important critique of the dominant culture's ideas and values. In every case they contributed to society by providing havens to the disenchanted, very often the most creative people in society. All societies—including communist societies—have such countercultures, which often provide the beginning of criticisms that lead to social change.

The term *group culture* is sometimes used to refer to a culture that arises in a group or formal organization. Like subculture and counterculture, group culture is a useful concept. The Los Angeles Lakers has a group culture, as does the First Lutheran Church and the Student Senate. Although not as distinct as a subculture, a group culture still has its own emphases and makes its members at least slightly different from outsiders.

In spite of these distinctions, it is more important to see that there is a basic similarity among all cultures. All of these are social patterns that arise in interaction. Every social organization has its own culture to some extent. Each is different from every other one, sometimes slightly, sometimes greatly so. Each has an important influence on the individual members.

CULTURE IS IMPORTANT

Culture is central to the individual and to social organization. First, *it influences what we do.* We worship God or worship gods or worship nothing because of our shared truths and norms and values: our culture. Americans may be materialistic, but that is not inherent to our nature. It arises from culture, which places a high value on material goods and causes us to make decisions that are materialistic. We marry, have children, get a job, buy a new home because that is what our culture causes us to do. And if we decide not to marry, not to have children, not to find a permanent job or buy a new home, that too can be linked to culture: to a culture that has changed over the past thirty years, causing many more of us to make such decisions. And we are controlled not only by American culture, but also by the cultures in our community, our formal organizations, our groups, and our dyads.

Second, *culture is important for social organization.* It is one of two patterns in all social organization (the other is structure). It means that those in interaction understand each other and agree with each other, they share a notion of what the world is all about and how they should work together in that world. We know what to expect from each other because of sharing culture; we become accustomed to each other's actions and ways of thinking. As a result we are able to cooperate, to problem solve together, to work things out.

Most people do not appreciate the power of culture. This is because the worlds we find ourselves in seem natural, proper, right, normal. It becomes, as some call it, a world taken for granted. Our culture's truths become ours, and it is difficult to understand why others can be so different, why others do things which are strange, why others seem to not want the same things we do, or why they just "think funny." And indeed, it is easy to understand why organizations benefit from teaching that their cultures are right and that other ways of doing things are wrong or silly or unnatural or sinful.

THE REAL SIGNIFICANCE OF CULTURE: "THE SOCIAL CONSTRUCTION OF REALITY"

It is easy to get lost in the many details contained in this chapter. It is easy to overlook the whole significance of culture when we try to memorize a number of subpoints.

The real significance of culture is that human beings come to believe what they do through interaction. Our truths, morals, values, and goals are, to a very great extent, socially created. This is an important insight, and it is often difficult to grasp. This is because every social organization attempts to make it appear that its culture and institutions are right, are in fact the only way "good people" should think or act. Social scientists sometimes call this tendency *ethnocentrism*, thinking that one's own culture (*ethno*) is central (*centrism*) to the universe, and that all other cultures are to be judged accordingly, usually as inferior.

In fact, once we appreciate the meaning of culture, it becomes difficult to be ethnocentric, to regard our own truths in absolute terms. Some of them may in fact be absolutely true, our values and morals may be absolutely right, but we can never know that for sure. All we can know for sure is that, to a great extent, what we have come to know and believe about the universe has resulted from interaction. It is cultural.

Reality may exist "out there," independent of how we see it. There may be something out there. However, how we see it, what we think about it, what we value in it, what we regard as right has arisen from what Peter Berger and Thomas Luckmann (1966) have called "the social construction of reality." It is through our social life that we come to know what exists. It is through our social life that we learn what is real, what to call it, and how to use it. Between "reality as it is" and "reality as I see it" exists social organization and its culture, the social eyeglasses through which I look.

SUMMARY

In this chapter we have emphasized that all social organizations develop the social pattern we have here called *culture.* Culture is a shared view of reality, a shared perspective, a shared agreement concerning what is true, right, and worthwhile. Culture, like social structure, arises in interaction, influences the individual actor, and helps assure social organization.

One more social pattern should be explained. That is the social pattern called *institution,* and it will be the subject of Chapter 7.

QUESTIONS TO CONSIDER

1. Explain how social structure and culture are alike. Explain how they are different.
2. What is culture, according to this chapter? How does this definition differ from other definitions you have learned?
3. What are the most important ideas you believe in? What are the most important values? What are the most important norms? Are these cultural?
4. Exactly what do social scientists mean when they say human beings are cultural animals?
5. Most of us want to believe that the cultures we share are true and good and that other cultures are probably not as good. Is there any way of establishing that one culture is in fact better than another?
6. What are the most important ideas people in the United States believe? What are the most important values? What are the most important norms we follow?

RECOMMENDED READING

The following are good introductions to culture in groups and formal organizations:

BECKER, HOWARD S. 1961. *Boys in white.* Chicago: University of Chicago Press.
COSER, LEWIS. 1974. *Greedy institutions.* New York: Free Press.
FINE, GARY ALAN. 1979. Small groups and culture creation. *American Sociological Review* 44: 733–745.
KEISER, R. L. 1969. *Vice lords: Warriors of the street.* New York: Holt, Rinehart & Winston.
LOFLAND, JOHN. 1966. *Doomsday cult.* 2d ed. Englewood Cliffs, N.J.: Prentice-Hall.
ROBERTS, KEITH A. 1978. Toward a generic concept of counter-culture. *Sociological Focus* 11: 111–116.

The following are good introductions to culture in communities and society:

BALDWIN, JAMES. 1963. *The fire next time.* New York: Dial Press.
BELLAH, ROBERT N., RICHARD MADSEN, WILLIAM M. SULLIVAN, ANN SWIDLER, and STEVEN M. TIPTON. 1985. *Habits of the heart: Individualism and commitment in American life.* New York: Harper and Row.
BENEDICT, RUTH. 1961. *Patterns of culture.* Boston: Houghton Mifflin.
BERGER, PETER L., and THOMAS LUCKMANN. 1966. *The social construction of reality.* Garden City, N.Y.: Doubleday.
BLUMBERG, PAUL. 1980. *Inequality in an age of decline.* New York: Oxford University Press.
DURKHEIM, EMILE. [1915] 1954. *The elementary forms of religious life.* Trans. Joseph Swain. Glencoe, Ill.: Free Press.
ERIKSON, KAI. 1976. *Everything in its path.* New York: Simon & Schuster.
GANS, HERBERT. 1967. *The Levittowners: Ways of life and politics in a new suburb.* New York: Pantheon.
GEHLEN, ARNOLD. 1980. *Man in the age of technology.* New York: Columbia University Press.
HOSTETLER, JOHN A., and GERTRUDE ENDERS HUNTINGTON. 1980. *Amish society.* 3d ed. Baltimore: Johns Hopkins University Press.
JONES, LANDON Y. 1980. *Great expectations: America and the baby boom generation.* New York: Coward, McCann and Geoghegen.
KANTER, ROSABETH. 1972. *Commitment and community.* Cambridge, Mass.: Harvard University Press.
KLUCKHOHN, CLYDE. [1949] 1957. *Mirror for man.* New York: McGraw-Hill.
LIEBOW, ELLIOT. 1967. *Tally's corner.* Boston: Little, Brown.
OLSEN, MARVIN. 1978. *The process of social organization.* New York: Holt, Rinehart & Winston.
ROSZAK, THEODORE. 1969. *The making of a counter culture.* New York: Doubleday.
SLATER, F. 1976. *The pursuit of loneliness.* Rev. ed. Boston: Beacon Press.
SUMNER, WILLIAM GRAHAM. [1906] 1940. *Folkways.* Boston: Ginn.
WEBER, MAX. [1905] 1958. *The Protestant ethic and the spirit of capitalism.* Trans. Talcott Parsons. New York: Scribner's.
WHITE, LESLIE. 1959. *The evolution of culture.* New York: McGraw-Hill.
WHITE, LESLIE, and B. DILLINGHAM. 1973. *The concept of culture.* Minneapolis: Burgess.
WILLIAMS, ROBIN. 1970. *American society: A sociological interpretation.* New York: Knopf.
ZBOROWSKI, M. 1953. Cultural components in responses to pain. *Journal of Social Issues* 8: 16–31.

The Senate (1935) by William Gropper. Oil on canvas. 25 ⅛ x 33 ⅛ inches. Collection, The Museum of Modern Art, New York. Gift of A. Conger Goodyear. Reprinted with permission.

7

The Institution

A THIRD SOCIAL PATTERN IN SOCIETY

A social structure is made up of a set of positions, all of which relate to one another. A culture is a shared reality that governs all actors in organization. An institution is *a type of action, interaction, or organization that is especially important to society.* It is a pattern that acts as a guide, an important norm that tells all of us how things are to be done in society. It is a central value—it is very important to most of us—and we feel obligated to defend it, even fight for it. It is also an important truth to us, since most of us most of the time regard it as the only right way to do things in society (this is how normal or moral people act).

Think of an institution as a *groove,* an important pattern in society that we learn to follow, which directs many of our actions. It is easy to confuse a social organization and an institution. My family is an organization; *the monogomous family is an American institution.* General Motors is a social organization; *the large corporation is an American institution.* The University of Arizona is a social organization; *the university is an American institution.* These institutions are the way we do things in our society; they are influential in the types of organizations we develop and the types of actions we all take.

The term "institution" is used in many ways. Sometimes the

president of my university likes to address a gathering with "this institution of higher learning, Moorhead State University." But in the strict sense we are using here, Moorhead State is not an institution, but a formal organization. The word institution is often applied to an organization in order to give the organization importance, permanence, legitimacy, and inevitability in the eyes of others.

INSTITUTIONS ARE WIDELY ACCEPTED AND DEEPLY ENTRENCHED

To extend our definition, we might say that *an institution is a type of action, interaction, or organization which has become widely accepted and appears to be a natural pattern in society*—the only sensible way for people to do something. Institutions regulate people's behavior by determining courses of action for them that they follow without seriously considering an alternative. Most animals are governed by instincts, humans are governed by institutions. Marriage is an institution. People do not have to get married—but in our society that is the accepted, legitimate, right, moral, even healthy way that people are supposed to live. Marriage is more than a simple norm—it is a widely followed pattern, and alternatives, at least until recently, were considered less than desirable. There are many other examples of ways of doing things that appear as the only way—the right way: capitalism, the corporation, the public school, private health care, woman's role as housewife, the secular state, federalism, professional athletics. These are all American institutions—the way we do things in this society, the way we expect things to be done, patterns that are considered by most to be the way America works.

The point emphasized here is that *institutions are entrenched and important normative patterns that establish how people are supposed to act in society.* They are cultural norms, but they are *the most important norms,* and they are widely accepted. There is a widely shared belief that the institution has no alternatives, that doing something else is strange, wrong, or whatever. Institutions are part of our taken-for-granted world. We think that "everyone does it that way," when indeed it is only because of shared agreement that people have come to adopt a particular alternative. It really did not "have to be" that way.

Segregation, for example, has long been an institution in our society. The famous black author James Baldwin wrote to his nephew concerning segregation in this country:

> Try to imagine how you would feel if you woke up one morning to find the sun shining and all the stars aflame. You would be frightened because it is out of the order of nature. Any upheaval in the universe is terrifying because it so profoundly attacks one's sense of one's reality. Well, the black man has functioned in the white man's world as a fixed star, as an immovable pillar: and as he moves out of his place heaven and earth are shaken to their foundations....(1963, 23)

When an institution such as segregation begins to crumble, many people find their taken-for-granted world shaken. When the legal basis for segregation was challenged, many fought hard to prevent it. When segregated schools and segregated lunch counters were challenged, many cried out that civilization was finally ending. When busing to achieve integrated schools was instituted in various communities, and where organizations were forced to institute affirmative action procedures, many argued that our democracy was on the way out. We are all used to institutions, and the institution of segregation is one. People fight to maintain what they are used to, and it is very difficult for them to understand that other ways of doing things may be more legitimate, more rational, or more humane. Institutions are like "fixed stars," "immovable pillars."

An institution is *a normative pattern that has taken a long time to develop*—it is anchored in history—and this is what makes it seem natural and aids its widespread acceptance.

When something has been around for a long time, it seems to be important. Institutions are patterns that are viewed by people in society as generally important: *Important for the continuation of society.* The presidency, voting, and the two-party system are social patterns we regard as central to our political order. What would our society be without marriage, monogamy, romantic courtship? What would we be without the large corporation, fast food, automobiles, and television? Such patterns are central to what we are as a society: They are action patterns—the way we do things—we call institutions.

THE MEANING OF INSTITUTION: A SUMMARY

To be considered an institution, then, a pattern must meet certain criteria. We might think of an institution as existing on one side of a continuum: The more closely a pattern meets all the criteria, the more it can be considered an institution (Figure 7–1).

A pattern may have a long history, yet it may be seen as one possible alternative among many (college education, for example)— it is not fully an institution. Or a pattern may be widely accepted but not really considered right, natural, or necessary (a custom such as wearing jeans), so it, too, does not fully meet the criteria of an institution. Heterosexuality is an excellent example of a pattern of behavior that comes close to fully meeting the criteria. It has a long history of acceptance, it has been long regarded as the only legitimate kind of sex activity, it is regarded as right and natural, and it is viewed as central to the continuation of society. In our society, Christianity is a good example of an institution, as is the secular state with its separation of church and state. We now have a volunteer army, but this does not seem to have gained institutional

FIGURE 7–1   Criteria for an Institution, which Exist on a Continuum

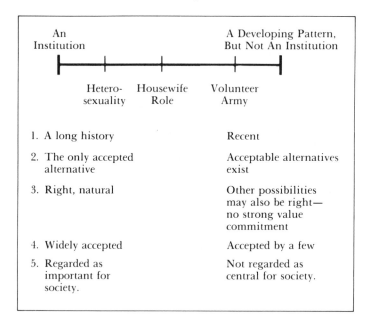

An Institution	A Developing Pattern, But Not An Institution
Hetero- Housewife Volunteer sexuality Role Army	
1. A long history	Recent
2. The only accepted alternative	Acceptable alternatives exist
3. Right, natural	Other possibilities may also be right— no strong value commitment
4. Widely accepted	Accepted by a few
5. Regarded as important for society.	Not regarded as central for society.

stature. It is recent, it is but one alternative, and it is not regarded as necessarily the right way to handle the problem of a standing army. Television, on the other hand, has increasingly approached institutional status in American life during the last twenty years.

IMPORTANCE OF INSTITUTIONS

Institutions are like social structure and culture. They are social patterns we learn, we generally accept, and we use to guide our decisions. These are the right ways we do things in this society. They are grooves that tell us how to raise our children, how to spend our leisure time, how to participate in government, and how to deal with death. From the standpoint of the individual, institutions are controls.

From the standpoint of society, institutions exist in order to assure that problems are successfully dealt with. Institutions are the many ways society maintains order, socializes people to accept the social patterns, makes sure that people cooperate, keeps the economy working, and protects people from harm. Every society develops political institutions, legitimate ways of dealing with political problems. Every society develops its own kinship institutions, legitimate ways of dealing with childbearing, regulation of sex, socialization of children, and inheritance of property. Every society also develops economic, military, religious, and educational institutions, legitimate ways of dealing with other problems it faces.

Examples of kinship institutions include monogamy, marriage, the nuclear family, and the woman as housewife. We have traditionally handled kinship problems in our society through these institutions. Yet institutions today are changing rapidly. Divorce, for example, is increasingly an institution. It has become a widely accepted, legitimate way to handle problem marriages. The housewife is an institution that is also changing at a rapid pace as many question the traditional role for women in marriage. Indeed, marriage itself is no longer the institution it once was. Living together without being married, single parenthood, and open marriages are acceptable alternatives.

Political institutions include the two-party system, federalism, the American presidency, the federal income tax, and the Supreme

Court (notice that a status position and a formal organization have themselves become so central to American society as to become institutions). Some economic institutions are the corporation, mass advertising, the credit card, and market pricing. Examples of military institutions are the joint chiefs of staff, the U.S. military academy, and the armed forces. Religious institutions include Protestantism, Sunday school, and Christmas, while examples of educational institutions are the public school, the high school, the neighborhood school, and grading. Finally, entertainment institutions include television, professional sports, and private country clubs. Things don't have to be this way, but they are—these are the institutions that dominate this society.

Every people in their history develop patterns which help them work out the problems they must solve to exist as a society. The patterns that are developed and passed on are called institutions.

INSTITUTIONALIZATION—AND ITS OPPOSITE—IS A CONTINUING PROCESS

It is often difficult to conclude that a pattern of behavior is really an institution, because of the changing nature of society. Society's long-established institutions no longer seem to most of us to be the only acceptable way of doing things; alternatives are springing up, and the media publicize them. In some areas such as kinship we are experiencing "deinstitutionalization" to the point that there are choices to be made by each individual at every turn rather than one established path for all people to follow.

The terms *institutionalization* and *deinstitutionalization* are useful for describing the developing patterns in society. As a normative pattern becomes widely accepted, is seen as morally right, important for the society and for individuals, we say it is becoming institutionalized or it is becoming an institution. When it ceases to be important or dominant or the only alternative, either another normative pattern replaces it or that area of life becomes "deinstitutionalized." Deinstitutionalization may be good. It increases each person's options and alternatives in making decisions about what he or she wants. But it may also cause problems such as greater stress because of less guidance and less certainty of what to do, and it may mean less agreement and cooperation among people in society. Deinstitutionalization, like everything else in social organization, is a complex matter with both benefits and costs.

THE REJECTION OF SOCIAL INSTITUTIONS

Not all communities, formal organizations, groups, and dyads accept society's institutions, and many that develop their own alternative patterns come into conflict with the larger society. These may be political radicals, minorities, young people, or individuals seeking a different culture from what American society offers, such as artists, students, the religiously committed, and some who wish to maintain their ethnic group heritage. Sometimes alternative patterns are left alone, but often the powerful in society see them as challenges and they are either outlawed or discouraged in more subtle ways. Among gay groups, for example, homosexuality is legitimate, but government, religion, and the police will in many communities join to declare homosexuality outside the accepted order. To some violence against police is acceptable, but to those in the larger society such acts are clearly illegitimate. Even stealing, cheating, or killing is legitimized by some groups, but such ways are usually seen as a threat to dominant institutions and dealt with accordingly. To most in the United States the English language is an institution, and those who speak another language are influenced to conform.

Some alternative patterns of behavior are therefore regarded as harmless, while others are defined as serious threats to the dominant institutions. But who decides what behavior is harmless and what must be discouraged or dealt with as serious challenges to the social order? Those who have high positions also have the power to define what is an institution, what is an acceptable alternative, and what is a threat. Sometimes "the people" may speak through elections or by other indirect means, and they may decide, say, that homosexuals should still be treated by authorities as illegitimate; sometimes an election can defeat a politician who attempts to institutionalize abortion; but in the long run institutions are determined by those who have power in society through either their positions or through the groups or formal organizations that have resources such as money or efficient organization to achieve their will.

SUMMARY

People interact. Over time they develop social patterns. Social structure and culture inevitably arise. Over time institutions also arise. Social structure positions us, and gives us role, identity, perspective, power, privilege, and prestige. Culture tells us what to believe; it gives us our truths, values, goals, and norms. Social institutions tell us how things are done in society: They are the widely accepted, legitimate, historical, important grooves that a society has developed to solve its problems. Figure 7–2 illustrates social organization and its social patterns.

One final point should be stressed. The conflict perspective in sociology reminds us that culture and institutions not only work to keep society together, they also work to maintain the social structure. Indeed, the culture and institutions that develop are to a great extent the products of those who are powerful in the social structure.

FIGURE 7–2   The Three Social Patterns within Social Organization

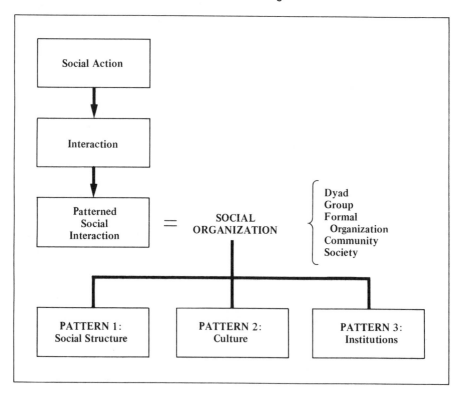

The housewife role, female passivity, the modern corporation, and the double standard used to judge sexual behavior—American institutions—reflect male power in society. American culture has been created by and for men, whites, and the wealthy, to a great extent. Instead of functioning just for the whole society, institutions and culture should also be understood as functioning for some at the expense of others.

In the conflict perspective, culture and institutions are embedded in social structure. They reflect and perpetuate the inequality that exists. They arise from conflict, and their existence reflects the interests of those who won in the conflict.

It is important to be balanced in our understanding: Institutions and culture are patterns we share, which solve our collective problems, which guide our lives, and which maintain organization. They are also patterns that favor those who have had most to do with their creation, those at the top of social structure.

QUESTIONS TO CONSIDER

1. What is an institution? Try to remember the various qualities that describe an institution.

2. List five political institutions, five economic institutions, and five educational institutions. List ten other institutions that are not primarily political, economic, or educational institutions.

RECOMMENDED READING

BELLAH, ROBERT N., RICHARD MADSEN, WILLIAM M. SULLIVAN, ANN SWIDLER, and STEVEN M. TIPTON. 1985. *Habits of the heart: Individualism and commitment in American life.* New York: Harper and Row.

BERGER, PETER L., and THOMAS LUCKMANN. 1966. *The social construction of reality.* Garden City, N.Y.: Doubleday.

CHIROT, DANIEL. 1986. *Social change in the modern era.* New York: Harcourt Brace Jovanovich.

CLOTFELTER, JAMES. 1973. *The military in American politics.* New York: Harper & Row.

COSER, LEWIS, and ROSE COSER. 1974. *Greedy institutions.* New York: Free Press.

DOMHOFF, G. WILLIAM. 1983. *Who rules America now?: A view for the 80s.* Englewood Cliffs, N.J.: Prentice-Hall.

MILLS, C. WRIGHT. 1956. *The power elite.* New York: Oxford University Press.

SCANZONI, LETHA DAWSON, and JOHN SCANZONI. 1988. *Men, women, and change.* 3d ed. New York: McGraw-Hill.

STARR, PAUL. 1982. *The social transformation of American medicine.* New York: Basic Books.

USEEM, MICHAEL. 1984. *The inner circle.* New York: Oxford University Press.

Metropolis (1923) by Paul Citroen. © Paul Citroen/VAGA, New York, 1989. Reprinted with permission.

8

The Interrelationships among Organizations

So far in this discussion we have focused on three patterns of social organization: social structure, culture, and institutions. Social structure means that people come to do things in relation to each other based on their positions. Culture means that people come to agree on matters of what is true, what things are worth working for, and which behavioral patterns are proper and right. An institution means an action pattern in society which has developed to deal with one of society's ongoing problems, a groove that we accept as right and true.

We should not lose sight of the fact that social structure, culture, and institutions are important for what the person does—all influence individual action. The individual should be understood as located in social organization, doing and thinking things expected in that location, and acting in ways that conform to the truths, values, goals, norms, and institutions.

SOCIAL ORGANIZATIONS INFLUENCE EACH OTHER

But an organization never develops in a vacuum; it must be understood in relation to all other organizations, and this makes analysis difficult. In a real sense we can identify each organization within a larger organizational structure, in a "position" with more or less power, privilege, and prestige than the others.

It is easiest to understand this when we look at American corporations. On close examination we find a definite structure among corporations, with certain financial giants like Morgan Trust playing a dominant role and others like Control Data and Xerox filling lower positions in the corporate world. There is structure among automobile companies, among oil companies, and among steel companies. There is also complex structure among automobile, oil, and steel companies together. Sociologists are beginning to document the extensive control by some financial organizations of other large corporations, the overlapping boards of directors of organizations, and the role of merger and conglomeration in the business world.

Educational organizations as well have positions in relation to each other. Some, like Harvard, have more power, privilege, prestige, and have a definite role, identity, and perspective within the academic world. And, of course, a college like Harvard will also have a position in the world of business, turning out people with degrees to fill positions in corporations, perhaps influencing those corporations, but also being heavily influenced by the corporations to turn out the "right kind of people." And the ties with government are also evident.

There is also structure among athletic teams, churches, gangs, and departments in colleges. There is a world structure consisting of societies, with each society coming to fill a position in the world system.

Structure, then, should be understood broadly. Not only does it include relations of individuals, but also relations among social organizations.

We can also see culture and institutions emerging among social organizations as individuals from each interact and come to share beliefs, values, norms, goals, and ways of handling ongoing problems. Societies become increasingly similar through interaction. Simple agricultural societies, for example, become industrialized and urbanized as they are drawn into the world community. A common culture emerges among colleges, among fashion designers, among manufacturers, and among communities as interaction takes place between leaders and members of these various organizations.

Every organization must be understood, then, in the context of its social environment—other organizations occupying positions and sharing culture and institutions in interaction. Figure 8–1 illustrates this mutual influence. The problem of the sociologist is to understand the nature of these relationships. Within the automobile industry there is interaction and there is an emerging social structure, with General Motors and Ford dominating. Chrysler took

FIGURE 8–1   The Automobile Industry and Emerging Social Patterns

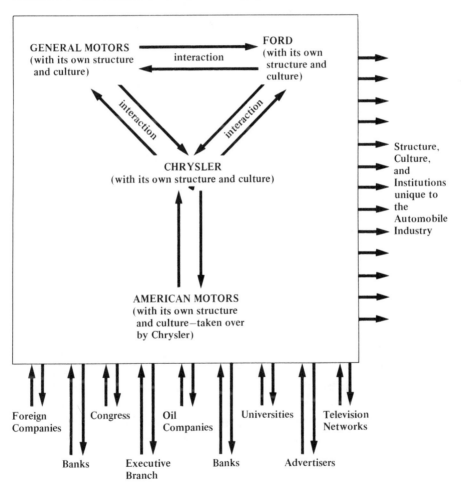

over American Motors and is competing for dominance. The industry has positions for each company, with power, prestige, and privilege. Over time all within the industry are influenced to share a view of foreign competitors, air pollution, the value of the automobile to American life, American capitalism, and American universities. Together they influence Congress and other corporations. In their hiring practices they communicate to the universities the kinds of people needed to fill the industry, and in their advertising campaigns they influence the kinds of programs they are willing to support on television. Of course, they are not all-powerful. The relationships are highly complex. Television, banking practices, and decisions made by oil companies have impact on the automobile industry too. The point is, however, that a relationship exists: There is interaction, structure, emerging culture, and the nature of all of this must be documented in order to understand the nature of the automobile industry in the United States.

SOCIAL ORGANIZATIONS ARE EMBEDDED IN LARGER SOCIAL ORGANIZATIONS

Furthermore, the interrelationships can be extended to include the fact that each *level* of social organization—dyad, group, formal organization, community, and society—is embedded in and influenced by larger levels of social organization. My family is located in Atlanta, Georgia. Atlanta is located within American society. What develops in my family is influenced by the patterns in the United States and in Atlanta. The structure and size of my family depends on the nature of the family in American life in the 1990s. Atlanta differs in ways from the rest of American society, so the nature of my family will be influenced by that also. How I relate to my wife and my children is not developed in a social vacuum; the patterns we develop are influenced by larger social organization. Spanking children is a good way to discipline children—or is it a poor way?—or is it child abuse? How my wife and I define it depends on my community and society, at least to some extent. The role expectations I have for my wife depend, in part, on the social worlds we live within. I encourage my children to try baseball, football, or dancing depending in part on my community. The social patterns of any social organization must always be considered in the context of larger social organization (Figure 8–2).

Here is an interesting phenomenon: American society affects us directly by placing us in and teaching us its structures, culture, and institutions, but it also influences us indirectly through other social organizations. Its institutions, for example, influence the kinds of businesses, families, and schools that develop in communities. Indeed, its structures and culture influence the kinds of communities that develop. Its stratification system influences our groups—who interacts with whom, who marries whom, and all the patterns of group behavior. You and I—well, we are individuals located in social organization, who learn cultures, who fit into stratification systems and structures, and who fit into the multitude of patterns that have developed for such a long time. Even if we try to develop our own dyad or group or formal organization, its patterns will be influenced, even determined, by the kinds of patterns that the society has laid out for it for such a long time.

SOCIETY WITHIN A WORLD ORDER

As interaction is facilitated throughout the world, we must also see societies embedded in an even larger entity. We live in a world system where travel, instant communication, trade, and colonialization create a worldwide social structure and culture. As societies become less isolated, they are influenced to become like others or they are influenced to change in order to make contributions to the others.

The multinational corporation facilitates this process. Labor, management, owners, and buyers in a corporation are no longer confined to a single society. The laborers of Hong Kong, the owners in New York, the managers in both Hong Kong and New York, and the customers in Africa all make up the modern corporate world.

This world order has power and inequality too. There is a worldwide social structure, with some societies having more power,

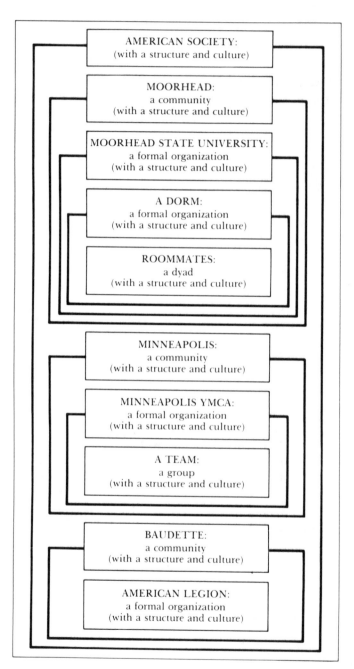

FIGURE 8–2 Levels of Social Organization Exist within Larger Levels of Social Organization

privilege, and prestige than the others. By 1900, Immanuel Wallerstein writes (1974), the world became both highly interdependent and dominated by Europe and the United States. The world was a source of inexpensive labor, raw materials, and agriculture. All societies changed as a result, but the poorer societies were changed to suit the needs of the more powerful societies. The powerful societies Wallerstein calls the "core societies"; they were the "center" of world power in 1900; the poorer societies Wallerstein calls "peripheral."

Understanding the social structure of the world today is very important for understanding relations among societies. That structure is far more complex than it was in 1900. Some peripheral nations have developed around the Soviet Union, which has become an important core society. The Western industrialized societies are still dominant throughout much of the world, but Great Britain less so since World War II, and the United States less so since 1970. Some countries, such as Brazil and China, are neither core nor peripheral societies (Wallerstein calls them semiperipheral). Many societies, once outright colonies of the Western world, have learned from the West, and, after gaining political independence, have tried to become more economically independent, with mixed success. Sometimes the Western societies have been replaced by dependence on the Soviet Union (Cuba, for example); sometimes the dependence on the West has been impossible to break (Latin America, much of Africa, much of Southeast Asia, for example); sometimes the lessons learned from the West have led to core society status (Japan, for example).

Interaction between societies changes all societies. Interdependence develops, the culture of each affects the cultures of the others, and the position of the society within the larger world order affects that society's structure, culture, and institutions.

SUMMARY

This chapter tries to show that social organizations never exist within a social vacuum. They are rarely on their own in the types of social patterns they develop. The individual is not only influenced by his or her face-to-face interaction; instead, larger and larger social forces influence the development of smaller and smaller organization.

Individual actors interact, form structures and culture in that interaction, and are in turn affected by those social patterns. That interaction and its resulting social patterns are influenced by larger groups, formal organizations, community, and society within which they exist. The individual and his or her dyads and groups should be understood within a set of concentric circles, each one having something to say about what occurs.

Interaction between people from different organizations develops social patterns among those organizations. A structure develops that positions those organizations in relation to one another. A culture is created that ties those organizations together. An individual organization must always be understood in terms of its position within these larger structures. This includes a world system where societies too interact, form a structure, and, to some extent, develop a common culture and common institutions.

QUESTIONS TO CONSIDER

1. Take a number of organizations you are familiar with—high schools or athletic teams in the same league or nations in the world. Place each in a position within a structure. Can you describe each organization's relative power, privileges, and prestige, as well as its identity, role, and perspective?

2. Take a dyad or small group that you are part of. Place it within larger and larger organizations. Exactly how do the larger organizations influence what goes on in your dyad or small group?

RECOMMENDED READING

BERGER, PETER L. 1963. *Invitation to sociology.* Garden City, N.Y.: Doubleday.
HALL, RICHARD. 1977. *Organizations, structure, and process.* 2nd ed. Englewood Cliffs, N.J.: Prentice-Hall.

PERROW, CHARLES. 1986. *Complex organizations: A critical essay.* 3d ed. New York: Random House.

WALLERSTEIN, IMMANUEL. 1974. *The modern world system.* New York: Academic Press.

Government Bureau by George Tooker. Egg Tempera on gesso panel.
19 ⅝ x 29 ⅝ inches. The Metropolitan Museum of Art, New York.
George A. Hearn Fund, 1956. Reprinted with permission.

9

Social Order, Social Control, and Social Deviance

Throughout this book we have examined the effects of social organization on the individual. It undoubtedly appears by now that the sociological perspective emphasizes the fact that human actors are controlled. For many students this is a disturbing realization. However, we must also look at this from the point of view of organization. Without some control over the individual, social organization simply would not exist. Society, a business organization, a university, an athletic team, or simply a group of children wanting to play "kick the can" would not exist if there were not some controls operating on the individual.

We are here introducing "the problem of order." Human cooperation is impossible without some degree of order. Society works because of order. The socialization of human beings works because of social order, and therefore the existence of human beings depends on social order. Even freedom—whatever there is—exists within some underlying order.

Social order—a concept often used but rarely defined—is a quality of all organization. The opposite of social order is easy to grasp: disorder, chaos, the absence of patterns, disorganization. The absence of social order means that actors act without taking others into account: Impulsive action or self-controlled action without concern for the whole prevails. Cooperation is made impossible.

The meaning of social order is more difficult to grasp, but if we begin with its opposites we can begin to understand this concept.

Social order means that social patterns successfully assure that interaction continues over time. Organization holds together, it is cohesive or integrated (social solidarity exists).

Where social order exists, actors know what to do, actors act with each other in mind and according to the social patterns developed. Actors control their own acts according to the rules of the organization. Where social order exists, cooperation is possible.

It is sometimes easy to be misled and think that social order is necessarily a good thing. Sometimes it is; sometimes it is not. An organization that values social order above all else becomes totalitarian (all-controlling). Too much social order discourages individuality, conflict, and change, also important aspects of organization.

SOCIAL ORDER IS ESTABLISHED
THROUGH STRUCTURE AND CULTURE

What makes order possible? How is it that we do not wake up one day to the absence of order? How does it hang on? There are societies that barely hang on, and formal organizations and groups that barely exist from day to day. But most organizations exist for a long time, and some have existed for centuries. How is order established so that individual actors know what to do and agree to act in ways consistent with the whole?

One reason is the social patterns themselves. Social patterns are guides to action; those guides control the actor; the actor acts in predictable and expected ways. These patterns bring people together, they make them interdependent, they even make them feel as one. Sociologists have described several ways that patterns help establish order and maintain continuous cooperative interaction.

Emile Durkheim (1893), for example, shows us how both culture and structure bind people. Culture is especially important in simpler societies. Here a common moral and value system binds people together. Durkheim called this "mechanical solidarity." People tend to be the same in such societies. Common beliefs, values, and norms are the glue. Crimes in such societies are regarded not as transgressions against other individuals so much as crimes against society and its common culture. Punishment and public executions serve to reaffirm this culture and give people the assurance that its truths, values, and morals are right. The worship of a common God and other sacred objects (objects that are symbolic of society) is also important, for, according to Durkheim, this too serves to hold people together and assure them that their culture is true. Durkheim called society's culture its "collective conscience" or "collective consciousness." The conscience (morality) and consciousness (awareness, understandings) of each individual are produced by the collective.

According to Durkheim, all societies have a common culture, and always this pattern holds societies together. Developed societies—particularly modern industrial societies—create complex social structures, where people take up different positions in society, and such differences between people replace the sameness that characterizes simpler societies. Industrial societies develop a complex "division of labor," where occupations are increasingly different from one another. We work at different jobs. We specialize. Some of us become corporate executives, some teach the families of corporate executives; some grow food, some transport it, and some prepare it for others. Such a society needs a common culture to some extent—after all, even if we are all different, we have to agree on some things or we would not be able to trust one another. However, it is a solidarity based on social structure which becomes increasingly important. Durkheim calls this "organic solidarity," because society increasingly takes the form of an organism with many different parts, each part making a contribution to the whole. Structure unites society by making us all *interdependent,* where human differences ultimately contribute to the needs of everyone. Without a common culture being central to social solidarity, and because people are increasingly different from one another, there is more tolerance of individuality and less severe punishment for those who break the law.

By contrasting mechanical solidarity with organic solidarity, Durkheim shows us how both culture and structure are important ingredients for holding society together, thus creating a sound basis for social order.

Marx too shows us the role of both structure and culture. His analysis is different from Durkheim's. He does not use the term social order but is more comfortable with the concept social *control.*

To Marx social control refers to the various ways the powerful in society attempt to repress the individual, to control and manipulate the individual for the good of the few. To Marx, society is a system of class inequality, and such inequality allows the few who own the means of production to coerce and manipulate the many to accept society as it is. Power in the social structure brings control over jobs, government, army, police, courts, and the media, and this, in turn, brings control over the individual. Therefore, Marx begins with social structure in his understanding of order: Order is produced through the power of a few people high in the social structure. They establish order through force, control of people's jobs, and manipulation.

Marx also deals with culture in his analysis of order. The dominant ideas, values, and morals in society are produced by the powerful. They are meant to control the individual to help assure "willing" conformity. Culture helps justify and protect the inequality in society, and it serves the powerful which produce it.

Thus, to Marx, social order is created from above. Position brings power; power brings the instruments that are used to create order so that privilege continues. Power also brings control over culture: a people's ideas, values, and rules.

Here then are two very different social thinkers, both of whom see the importance of social structure and culture to producing social order.

SOCIAL ORDER DEPENDS ON SOCIALIZATION

Order must also be understood as arising from the various attempts by every organization to get the individual to "willingly" conform, to leave all individuality at the door of organization, to accept the structure and culture as his or her own. Why are we so willing to do this?

"Willingness" arises from *socialization*, the third foundation for social order. It is through the process of socialization that social organization creates our wants, gives us its culture, and places us in our positions. Socialization refers to the process by which the individual is taught to know the society, to learn its culture and structure as well as his or her place there. Through socialization we learn to accept social organization because we are taught that it benefits us, or it *is* us, or we must accept it in order to survive. To become socialized is to "become" society, to make it part of us, to internalize it. Each social organization we enter and each we form sets up socialization procedures to make sure new members learn the patterns and assure that things work smoothly.

Consider what human beings are at birth, able to do little except depend on others. Human helplessness assumes a social nature. Immediately, adults begin to teach their infants who they are, where they fit into the family and society, what rules and values to act on. These lessons affect the children and direct them until gradually they become what they have been taught. Every society establishes institutions—for example, family, public schools, Sunday school, television, and the Boy Scouts—to socialize the young. We exist as a society in large part because socialization is successful:

> Every year our nation is invaded by several million "things" (one searches for the right word) that are immense, incalculable threats to the social order. They threaten total chaos. They are barbaric. They do not love democracy and suspect communism. They have no belief for the Judao-Christian tradition. They have no modesty. They do not speak our language, nor know our history, nor value our customs. They lack any motive or knowledge which leads them to share, to give and take, to compromise, to accommodate, to cooperate. They are impulsive and demanding. They do not respect authority, show respect to their elders, or express deference. Though they do not swear, steal, chew tobacco, fornicate, desecrate the flag, or use four-letter words, they are unaware certainly that they should not do so. They have no manners, no respect for others, no respect for tradition. They have not learned to keep up appearances, to knock before entering, to be silent in church, or to worry about bad breath and underarm stains.
>
> These invaders are human infants....Something must be done. We need them—because without them the society dies out for lack of people—but we need them on our terms, not theirs. The process of getting them on our terms is called *socialization*. (Campbell, 1975, 1)

The kinship institutions are very important for the socialization of a child. The family, the first group within which there is regular interaction, is made up of the first people the child uses as models, and it is the first source of rewards and punishments. The family is important for the emotional well-being of the child and central to the development of self and conscience. Because its teachings come first, the family influences all later learning. The adults confront the child with a world where alternatives do not seem to exist:

It is only much later that he discovers that there are alternatives to this particular world, that his parents' world is relative in space and time, and that quite different patterns are possible. Only then does the individual become aware of the relativity of social patterns and of social worlds. (Berger and Berger, 1972, 55–56)

The public school is an institution designed to socialize the young and create "good citizens." It attempts to teach ideas and actions that society (and those who have powerful positions in society) has determined are important. We are supposed to learn what America means, what history is, and why we should believe in its culture. Although many Americans believe that schools are the chief means for escaping low position in society, for the most part schools actually function to help people learn their place, to learn what it means to be a woman or man, black or white, rich or poor. Schools shape the individual's expectations of self and usually succeed in teaching people not to "expect too much." Malcolm X, an important black leader in the 1960s, described his experience in eighth grade, where Mr. Ostrowski, his English teacher, tried to influence Malcolm's expectations of himself:

He told me, "Malcolm, you ought to be thinking about a career. Have you been giving it thought?"

The truth is, I hadn't. I never have figured out why I told him, "Well, yes, sir, I've been thinking I'd like to be a lawyer." Lansing certainly had no Negro lawyers—or doctors either—in those days, to hold up an image I might have aspired to. All I knew for certain was that a lawyer didn't wash dishes, as I was doing.

Mr. Ostrowski looked surprised, I remember, and leaned back in his chair and clasped his hands behind his head. He kind of half-smiled and said, "Malcolm, one of life's first needs is for us to be realistic. Don't misunderstand me, now. We all here like you, you know that. But you've got to be realistic about being a nigger. A lawyer—that's no realistic goal for a nigger. You need to think about something you can be. You're good with your hands—making things. Everybody admires your carpentry shop work. Why don't you plan on carpentry? People like you as a person—you'd get all kinds of work."

The more I thought afterwards about what he said, the more uneasy it made me. It just kept treading around in my mind.

What made it really begin to disturb me was Mr. Ostrowski's advice to others in my class—all of them white....They all reported that Mr. Ostrowski had encouraged what they had wanted. Yet nearly none of them had earned marks equal to mine. (Malcolm X and Haley, 1964: 36–37)

It took Malcolm many years to understand his life and how it was shaped by many others. He turned against his early socialization because of people he interacted with later on. Many of us do not ever look back objectively at our socialization. We never do come to realize that much of it was an attempt by various representatives of society to get us to accept the social patterns that exist. Our taken-for-granted worlds appear to us as reality rather than as resulting from socialization.

No sociologist emphasizes the central role of schools more than Durkheim. Those organisms born into the world ignorant must be shaped, made into good citizens, and must go from being purely selfish to being cooperative and committed to the whole. To Durkheim, socialization or "moral education" takes society and its rules from existing "out there" and incorporates them into the individual's very being. This process internalizes the police force external to the individual, and the individual comes to direct self in accordance with society's demands. In all societies this is the task of the family and religion. In industrial society, this task is shared with the specialized educational institutions such as the public schools.

LOYALTY TO THE ORGANIZATION IS THE FOURTH FOUNDATION FOR SOCIAL ORDER

Socialization teaches us loyalty—being faithful to the group, organization, community, or society, and adhering to its beliefs. If the social organization can inspire people to feel part of something bigger than themselves, they will identify the organization with their own personal future, their own dreams, their own life's meanings. Societies develop loyalty in their members by waving their flags, marching their armies, displaying their heroes, and giving their speeches. Fraternities do it through initiation ceremonies, the frat house, secrecy, traditions. A ring, a marriage ceremony, a shared place of residence aid the development of loyalty to the marriage dyad. These symbols of loyalty distinguish insiders from outsiders, the in group from the out groups, "us" from "them." They encourage members to feel part of something good and to feel that they share this good with only certain selected others. An emotional bond is established, and this aids the smooth functioning of the organization.

Loyalty to the social organization may arise from two sources. Sometimes loyalty is a result of a sense of *we*, an emotional commitment to the organization which identifies the organization with one's own identity. This characterizes many smaller societies, communities, groups, and dyads. Cooley (1902) described such organizations as "primary"—those face-to-face relationships where a sense of *we* prevails and where personal emotional attachments exist. In such organization the individual identifies self with the whole, and personal goals are really organizational goals. An emotional commitment exists among all those in the organization.

It is difficult to establish a sense of *we* in large organization. Nations celebrate independence day, presidents give speeches to "my fellow Americans," and schools teach us about the great heroes and stirring events of our history. Wars sometimes bring us together as a nation, at least temporarily, as do national crises such as assassinations of public officials. Formal organizations may sponsor social events to encourage emotional attachment, or they might publish weekly staff newspapers announcing the promotions, achievements, recent hiring, and general office gossip. Christmas parties and bowling teams also help bring us together and establish emotional ties to the organization.

In modern society loyalty is often established through a second source: The organization must give us something in return. Even the family and friendship groups depend on conditional loyalty, more a rational commitment than an emotional one. Instead of a sense of *we*, a sense of *I* is most important. It is what society does for *me* that matters, it is whether or not my family meets *my* needs, whether this company looks out for *my* interests, whether this club gives *me* pleasure that determines my loyalty. Loyalty depends, it is conditional, it fluctuates, it is fickle. Much of our socialization into modern society is aimed at convincing us that as individuals we will get something in return for our loyalty.

Loyalty to social organization is aided by our social nature. Humans need other people in their early years for survival, and most of us need other people through most of our lives for our sense of worth. Almost all of us seek friends and have a need to be part of a group, a formal organization, a community, or a society. To be alone is something most of us fear. Others fulfill our emotional needs, and we develop our identities in group life. We want to give loyalty to the social organizations that are important for fulfilling our emotional needs; we are willing to sacrifice some of our individuality. Indeed, for most of us loyalty does not seem to be a sacrifice at all. Some of us hunger for being part of something larger than ourselves so much that we are willing to give up all individuality—we may, for example, join a religious or political movement that demands total loyalty.

Organizations also encourage loyalties through establishing boundaries between those in the organization and those outside. The structure and the culture act as boundaries distinguishing members from nonmembers. They control interaction through cutting ties with outsiders and encouraging interaction only with members of the organization. The ways of our group come to be seen as better than the ways of others, perhaps as the only desirable ways.

Organizations often manufacture physical and symbolic boundaries to encourage a sense of loyalty. A college campus is a set of buildings set apart from the rest of the community; a house acts as a physical boundary, as do a nation's borders, a factory, a membership card, a written contract. Physical boundaries help establish who "we" are and who "they" are. They encourage interaction among members and discourage interaction with outsiders. Symbolic boundaries such as uniforms, rings, football teams, theme songs, national anthems, and hair styles may establish boundaries too. Stereotyping others, calling them uncivilized, heathen, communists, uncool are ways some of us try to establish boundaries. Segregating others, creating ghettoes, passing discriminatory laws also do this.

To sum up, social order is established through four ways:

1. Social structure places us, makes us interdependent, and/or encourages control of the many by the few.

2. Culture makes people similar to one another in their truths, values, goals, and rules they follow.

3. Institutions socialize us so that society gets inside of us and we become "willing" partners in society.

4. Institutions encourage us to feel part of organization. Loyalty is encouraged, through developing a sense of we, through convincing members that the organization is beneficial, and through establishing boundaries between those within and those outside of the organization.

There is a fifth and final way, however, that social order is established, and we have not yet considered it. This is what sociologists call the use of social controls (or social sanctions). Put simply, if an actor follows the patterns he or she is rewarded; if an actor does not follow the patterns he or she is punished. All social organizations have ways to deal with actors who agree to conform, and those who do not wish to conform at all.

SOCIAL CONTROLS CONTRIBUTE
TO SOCIAL ORDER

Socialization is never perfect, loyalty for many is never felt, and the patterns for some are not willingly followed. This is true in society, in the university, and in all groups everywhere. If socialization worked perfectly there would be no criminals, no deviants, no revolutionaries, no dissatisfied members, no one unhappy with the social structure. To encourage reluctant members, social organizations always develop social controls. *Social controls are positive and negative social sanctions*—rewards and punishments—that operate within social organization to encourage conformity. Social controls alone do not usually guarantee conformity, but they are strong incentives for it. It is almost impossible for most organizations to function if they rely mainly on social controls, but it is also impossible for them to function without any social controls.

We are all familiar with negative sanctions—the pressures applied to bring people back in line if they stray. We can all stretch our status positions some; we can also be individuals within culture but only to a certain extent. Beyond a certain point people frown at us, they reject us, they yell at us, they embarrass us, they imprison us, they threaten to throw us out, they point a finger or a fist or a gun at us. We may conform to social organization out of fear that negative sanctions will be applied if we do not. The ultimate sanction is being thrown out of the social organization (imprisonment, expulsion, deportation, or execution). It is the bottom line.

Positive sanctions reward us if we do conform. A smile, a raise in salary, an A in a class, a compliment, a promotion, a medal of honor, a birthday present, all work to encourage acceptance of position, structure, and culture. Even thinking about future rewards encourages conformity.

Indeed, socialization is so effective in society that social controls become internalized. We come to exert our own social controls, we are our own policeman, so to speak. Sometimes we feel guilty and punish the self; at other times we feel good and pat ourselves on the back. External social controls become internal ones, society out there gets in us. Socialization, then, causes us to become our positions, to believe in our cultures, and to aid society in policing ourselves.

Human beings are pushed around, in a sense. We are told what to do; we are rewarded and we are punished. In any social situation sanctions are promised, threatened, and used. We must please many people, and we should probably face the fact that many of our claims of "free choice" are probably wishful thinking:

> The individual who, thinking consecutively of all the people he is in a position to have to please, from the Collector of Internal Revenue to his mother-in-law, gets the idea that all of society sits right on top of him had better not dismiss that idea as a momentary neurotic derangement. (Berger, 1963, 78)

THE MEANING OF SOCIAL CONTROL

The individual who is part of any social organization is, to some extent, a prisoner. The patterns of structure and culture influence our action, our thinking, and our very being. There is, in a sense, almost a conspiracy operating. Almost all elements in our social life act to *control* us, to alter our individual desires, at least slightly, so that society can continue.

The concept in sociology that describes all this is appropriately called *social control*. Social control (not to be confused with social controls, discussed previously) is a general term that refers to all the ways by which society—or any social organization—attempts to bring about individual conformity.

Roucek defines social control as "all the pressures by which society and its component groups influence the behavior of the individual members toward conformity with group norms" (1978, 11). As Figure 9-1 illustrates, social control is accomplished through everything discussed thus far: through structure, which places the individual; through culture, which makes the individual similar to others; and through institutions, which socialize, establish loyalty,

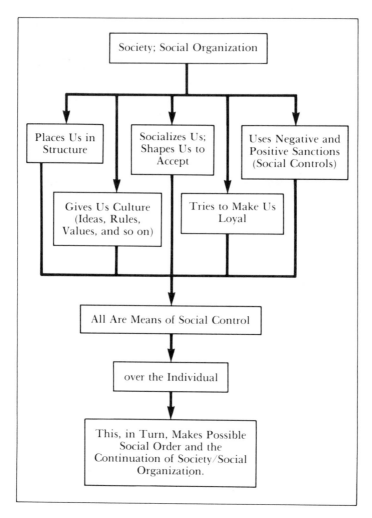

FIGURE 9–1   Social Control Is Accomplished through Structure, Culture, Institutions

and reward and punish the individual. All of these together are society's means of social control; all means of social control are ultimately the way that social order is established.

SOCIAL DEVIANCE

It is impossible to assure total conformity to organization, nor is that ever desirable. Society needs thinkers, not robots; problem solvers, not sleepwalkers; creative, self-directing persons, not simply conformists. Everyone breaks the established rules occasionally, and some break the rules much of the time. As children, we learn to test adults: We bend the rules of authorities, they act back, we test again. In real life everything is dynamic and involves conflict.

The problem is always *how much* individuality is acceptable? How much bending of the rules can be tolerated? Americans value individuality; yet we all have our limits, and certainly authorities do. Every social organization draws lines and brings negative social controls to bear on those outside those lines. High schoolers recognize well that there are certain acceptable ways to dress and act around peers; outsiders are nerds, uncool, queer. Certain people we declare to be mentally ill; others we punish as criminals. Wherever there are social patterns there are those who are unacceptable, who are condemned as "immoral," "sick," "criminal," "unnatural," or "antisocial."

Deviance is the name given by sociologists to that action regarded by society to be outside the range of the acceptable. Deviance in a sense is created by society, not the actor, since society makes the rules and draws the lines. Erich Goode defines deviance as follows:

> ...by *deviance* I mean one thing and one thing only: *behavior that some people in a society find offensive and which excites—or would excite if it were discovered—in these people disapproval, punishment, condemnation, or hostility*....It is based on a judgment made by somebody. It isn't simply behavior, but behavior that is evaluated in a certain way. (1978, 24–25)

Goode makes his point through the example of homosexuality. Is homosexuality deviant? Many people call it an illness, something that is "unnatural," something that is deviant *in itself,* not just because we say it is. But Goode is consistent with his definition. It is deviant *only* because of our reactions, our perception that it is a violation of something we believe in (1978, 376–377).

Labeling something deviant is really trying to exercise social control over people. Such labels stigmatize the individual and attempt to discourage such acts. Labeling also socializes people: To stray from the acceptable means that you, too, might be stigmatized.

Not all individuality can be condemned. Not everyone who strays can be punished. All societies are selective. Those who are condemned tend to be those who through their acts *threaten* us. Revolutionary acts threaten powerful groups, illegal acts threaten those who perceive the law to be important to their welfare, "weird" religious cults threaten those who view God and life in a more traditional way, and "kinky" sex threatens those of us who regard more traditional acts to be a healthy and moral way. Where we condemn acts as deviant (not just different), there is something important at stake for us.

Deviance is universal; however, each society has a different view of what is deviant, and that changes from generation to generation. Even when it might appear that almost all societies agree on some general category of action as deviant (e.g., murder or incest), careful examination will show that they differ in their definitions of what specific acts are to be included in the category.

Deviant acts are sometimes written into the law. Where laws are passed and punishment for violation is relatively severe (rather than, for example, simply a fine), we have instances of deviance having become a "crime." Some deviant acts—for example, those we see arising from mental illness—are considered deviant in this society, not criminal. For a long time divorce was considered deviant, but not criminal.

Society is made up of many organizations who have different views of deviance. To pro-choice groups, pro-life groups are wrong, anti-woman, fanatical, and irrational. To pro-life groups, pro-choice groups are anti-life, immoral, anti-family, and murderers. Whose definition prevails? If we realize that society is made up of a number of groups in conflict, and that each group asserts itself with the power resources available to it, then it is easy to see that power makes a big difference in society's definition of deviance. Money, leadership, and organization matter; friends in Congress matter; control over schools and media matters. Clearly, the upper class has more say than others in what crimes are most serious (and these turn out to be more regularly the crimes most often committed by the lower classes). Mothers Against Drunk Driving in a very short time has influenced political leaders, judges, and the public to regard drunk driving as a deviant act to be harshly condemned. Leadership, organization, and intelligent use of the media were important sources of power that paid off for this group. Heterosexuals in society define homosexuality as criminal or "sick," and this will continue so long as the power of the homosexual community is not great enough to change it.

Almost any act, then, can be defined as deviant and persecuted.

Power differences create priorities in society, which then become reflected in the law and court system, and in our punishments.

The condemnation of certain acts as deviant and certain people as deviants are ways that authorities attempt to establish social order. Condemnation is itself a negative social control. It attempts to maintain structure and culture, it socializes the population as to what is acceptable, and sometimes it even helps bring the community together. In condemning others people can become more and more convinced that their rules are right, their truths correct, and their social organization superior to others.

Clearly, however, widespread deviance brings conflict, sometimes disorder, and almost always social change. Widespread violent crime brings fear and heightens distrust of the rules, of the authorities, and of other people. It threatens our taken-for-granted social patterns. Large social movements—for example, the civil rights movement, the feminist movement, the anti-Vietnam War movement—question the very nature of society, stretch and sometimes break the rules, challenge the authorities, and are almost always labeled deviant as they engage in organized action. Conflict and disorder almost always bring social change, sometimes slight, sometimes dramatic.

SUMMARY

Deviance underlines so well the fact that society and people are far more complex and dynamic than the earlier chapters of this book indicated. People are not simply located, socialized, controlled, passive actors. They decide to shape their roles, to say no to their socializers, to go in directions never intended by authorities.

Yet, what a mistake it is to ignore the concepts of social order and social control. Each social organization—from dyad to society—establishes means by which it attempts to control its members and establish social order. The patterns of structure and culture help guarantee order, as do socialization procedures, the encouragement of loyalty, and social controls. The condemnation of certain acts and people as deviant is probably the best example of how organization uses negative social controls. Deviance should be thought to be acts of people regarded as threatening to the continuation of social organization. Condemnation benefits social order; widespread deviance may challenge it and often is an important source of social change.

QUESTIONS TO CONSIDER

1. What is the meaning of "social order"? Can you think of an organization you know of that lacks social order? If so, describe what happens in such an organization.
2. What is the meaning of "social control"? How does it relate to social order?
3. What is the meaning of "social deviance"?
4. Deviance is universal, yet what societies call deviance is not. Is this true?
5. There are many ways that social order is achieved. We described five in this chapter: social structure, culture, socialization, loyalty, and social controls. Examine your own university, and show how each of these contributes to social order.

RECOMMENDED READING

The following works concern themselves with questions of social control and social order:

BECKER, HOWARD S., E. C. HUGUES, and B. GEER. 1961. *Boys in white.* Chicago: University of Chicago Press.

BERGER, PETER L. 1963. *Invitation to sociology.* New York: Doubleday.

BERGER, PETER L., and BRIGITTE BERGER. 1972. *Sociology: A biographical approach.* New York: Basic Books.

BERGER, PETER L., and THOMAS LUCKMANN. 1966. *The social construction of reality.* New York: Doubleday.

BREED, WARREN. 1955. Social control in the newsroom: A functional analysis. *Social Forces* 33: 326–335.

CAMPBELL, ERNEST Q. 1975. *Socialization, culture, and personality.* Dubuque, Iowa: W. C. Brown.

COOLEY, CHARLES HORTON. [1902] 1964. *Human nature and the social order.* New York: Schocken Books.

DURKHEIM, EMILE. [1893] 1964. *The division of labor in society.* Trans. George Simpson. New York: Free Press.

DURKHEIM, EMILE. [1895] 1964. *The rules of the sociological method.* Trans. Sarah A. Solovay and John H. Mueller. Glencoe, Ill.: Free Press.

DURKHEIM, EMILE. [1915] 1954. *The elementary forms of religious life.* Trans. Joseph Swain. Glencoe, Ill.: Free Press.

ELKIN, FREDERICK, and GERALD HANDEL. 1978. *The child and society.* 3d ed. New York: Random House.

EWEN, STUART. 1976. *Captains of consciousness.* New York: McGraw-Hill.
GOFFMAN, ERVING. 1961. *Asylums.* Chicago: Aldine.
MILGRAM, STANLEY. 1963. Behavioral study of obedience. *Journal of Abnormal and Social Psychology* 67: 371–378.
PETERS, THOMAS J., and ROBERT H. WATERMAN, JR. 1982. *In search of excellence.* New York: Warner Books.
ROSE, PETER I., ed. 1979. *Socialization and the life cycle.* New York: St. Martin's Press.
ROUCEK, JOSEPH. 1978. The concept of social control in American sociology. In *Social control for the 1980s,* ed. J. Roucek, 3–19. Westport, Conn.: Greenwood Press.
SHIBUTANI, TAMOTSU. 1961. *Society and personality.* Englewood Cliffs, N.J.: Prentice-Hall.
SHILS, EDWARD S., and MORRIS JANOWITZ. 1948. Cohesion and disintegration in the Wehrmacht in World War II. *Public Opinion Quarterly* 12: 280–294.
TOENNIES, FERDINAND. [1887] 1957. *Community and society.* Trans. Charles A. Loomis. East Lansing: Michigan State University Press.
TURNBULL, COLIN. 1972. *The mountain people.* New York: Simon & Schuster.

The following works are good introductions to the study of social control and deviance:

BECKER, HOWARD. 1973. *Outsiders.* Rev. ed. New York: Free Press.
BERGER, PETER L. 1963. *Invitation to sociology.* New York: Doubleday.
ERIKSON, KAI. 1966. *Wayward puritans: A study in the sociology of deviance.* New York: Wiley.
FINESTONE, HAROLD. 1976. *Victims of change.* Westport, Conn.: Greenwood Press.
GOODE, ERICH. 1978. *Deviant behavior: An interactionist approach.* Englewood Cliffs, N.J.: Prentice-Hall.
LEMERT, EDWIN M. 1967. *Human deviance, social problems, and social control.* Englewood Cliffs, N.J.: Prentice-Hall.
QUINNEY, RICHARD. 1980. *Class, state, and crime.* 2d ed. New York: Longman.
SILBERMAN, CHARLES. 1978. *Criminal violence, criminal justice.* New York: Random House.
X, MALCOLM, and ALEX HALEY. 1964. *The autobiography of Malcolm X.* New York: Grove Press.

Zapatistas (1931) by José Clemente Orozco. Oil on canvas. 45 x 55 inches. Collection, The Museum of Modern Art, New York. Given anonymously. Reprinted with permission.

10

Social Power

Bertrand Russell, a famous twentieth-century philosopher, put the matter better than anyone: "The fundamental concept in social science is Power, in the same sense in which Energy is the fundamental concept in Physics" (1938, 10).

Social power in many ways unites this whole book and is at the very heart of the sociological perspective. One cannot grasp how sociologists view reality without considering this concept.

Social power, like social order, is one of those words we all use but rarely define. In fact, the more we try to define it, the more the concept seems to elude us. Weber wrote that power has something to do with "achieving one's will," and that is a good place to begin. People who have power achieve their will in relation to others. When they want something they get it; they win in the relationship. Weber believed that social power accompanies social action, so, therefore, power is an element of a willful act, an intentional attempt to achieve one's will or to get one's way.

Actually, there are three ways to use the term power that make sense. Power is the *ability to achieve one's will*. It is potential. I have power to the extent that *I will be able in the future* to achieve my will in relation to others. Corporate executives have power: If they wish, they can achieve their will in government, in communities, in relation to employees. The United States has power in the world: If its leaders wish, they can achieve their will in relation to Israel, the

U.S.S.R., Egypt, or the United Nations. Some social scientists call power ability "potential power," the probability of achieving one's will *in the future.*

The second way the term power makes sense is to describe one's *actual power.* I have power to the extent that *I have already been successful* in achieving my will in relation to others. Corporate executives have power (actual power): In the past, they have been successful in achieving their will in relation to government, to communities, to employees. The United States has power in the world; it has successfully achieved its will in relation to Israel, the U.S.S.R., Egypt, and the United Nations.

The third way the term power is used is in the context of *trying to achieve one's will.* This we might call *exerted power.* Thus, corporate executives exert power when they try to get their way with government, communities, or employees. The United States exerts power in relation to Israel, the U.S.S.R., Egypt, and the United Nations.

Power, then, is a complex concept because it is used in many ways, three of which we have here described. To say that "someone has power" may mean either power ability or actual power; to say that someone "uses power" means that the actor exerts power.

To further clarify the meaning of power we might here introduce the concept "resources." *Resources include anything that an actor possesses that aids him or her to achieve will in a relationship.* Money is a resource, as is good organization, large numbers of people, an army, the police, the courts. Power ability depends on resources; the greater one's resources, the greater one's ability to get one's way. Actual power means that one has successfully used his or her resources. Exerted power is the use of resources in a relationship in order to achieve one's will.

Social power is involved in every instance of interaction. Whenever people interact, they will attempt to achieve their will in relation to the others. This can mean selling them something, influencing their views of the world, or controlling their actions. Whether or not they succeed depends on their resources, and it also depends on the resources of those with whom they are interacting. "I have more power than Elaine" means either that I can get my way if I want or that I have gotten my way in the past, or it can mean both.

Finally, we should briefly look at what it means to "get one's way" or to "achieve one's will." Normally, relationships are very complex, and no one gets his or her will completely. The outcome of exerting power is normally "influence," moving the others in the direction one desires. Sometimes it is "control," getting one's way without much resistance on the part of the others. We might put this on a continuum for clarification:

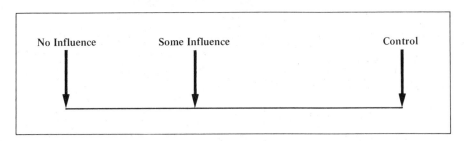

FIGURE 10–1   Outcomes of Exerting Power

The more control one has in a relationship, the more one is able to achieve his or her will.

The opposite of power is powerlessness. To be powerless means to be helpless in relation to others, to be determined by the will of others. Powerlessness means that one lacks control over one's own life, is unable to effectively resist the exertion of power by others, and lacks the ability to influence the direction of social organization, including society. Powerlessness brings dependence on others and exploitation (selfish use) by others, if they choose.

Whenever people interact they bring resources to that interaction. They each try to influence the direction of the interaction. There is always conflict, since each will have at least a slightly different goal. The greater their resources, the greater their potential power in the interaction. The more successful they are in the interaction, the more control—or actual power—they have in the relationship. If they lack resources, they are powerless; if they are powerless, then they are dependent on the other; if dependent, they can be exploited by the other; certainly they are controlled.

This is a model of power that we can apply to all types of social situations. It is a good beginning to understanding social power. Now, let us apply it to an understanding of social organization.

AUTHORITY

Amos Hawley wrote: "Every social act is an exercise of power, every social relationship is a power equation, and every social group or system is an organization of power" (1963, 422). Although for many of us power is something that sounds bad, it is an inherent part of all social life.

Earlier in this book we described the nature of social structure. Social structure is a network of social positions, each one of which has attached to it a certain amount of power. That is, *positions are resources.* They give the actors who fill them the ability to achieve their will. High position in organization brings influence or control over others in organization. When there is disagreement, those in high positions normally win. Of course, there are always other resources that can be brought to situations—money, intelligence, good looks, knowledge, physical strength, for example—but positions are of great importance wherever there is organization.

Max Weber's insights on authority are very important here. Weber pointed out that power can arise from many different bases, or resources. We might base our power on fear, money, or promises, for example. Nothing is as permanent and stable, however, as *authority:* position in organization regarded by others as *legitimate.* When rulers overthrow others, what do they immediately seek? Legitimacy. What do kings treasure? Legitimacy. What do revolutionary heroes work for? Legitimacy. In fact, parents, teachers, managers, and boards of directors carefully guard their legitimacy. Legitimacy is very important. It means, in essence, that someone (because of position in organization) has the *right to command others,* and others have *an obligation to obey.* In general, if one accepts his or her place in organization, one grants legitimacy to those above, and one claims legitimacy in relation to those below.

When people interact and they come to be placed into status positions, others in the organization come to get used to that structure, and all know what to do. As structure is formed, those positions become unequal—and again this comes to be accepted over time. Over time the tradition becomes a great ally, and those in organization, because they accept tradition, come to accept the inequality. Weber called such authority *traditional,* and pointed out, for example, that in highly traditional organization (such as in tribal societies), tradition determines who fills what position (usually determined by blood), and people simply accept what tradition commands. Therefore, those in high position have three important resources: position, tradition, and the organization itself. To disobey is to disobey position, tradition, and to be disloyal.

In the twentieth century traditional authority has overwhelmingly changed to *legal-rational authority*. This means that structure is written in the *law*. Positions are described in a constitution, and whoever fills those positions are given a right to command, and others feel an obligation to follow. Those in high position have three important resources: position, constitution/law, and the organization itself. To disobey is to disobey position, the law, and to be disloyal. Nations are founded on this, and almost every organization we enter today has elements of legal-rational authority, which makes power in organization stable over time, and business can be carried out without much difficulty.

Sometimes, Weber pointed out, there arises an extraordinary individual within society who gathers around him or her large numbers of people who regard that individual with great awe. This is *charismatic authority*. The individual, because his or her personal qualities are regarded as special, is granted legitimacy. People obey not because of tradition or law, but because of the magnetism of the individual, which is usually thought to be blessed by history or by the supernatural. Napoleon, Jesus, Ghandi, Martin Luther King, and Lenin are examples. Such people are revolutionary, and occasionally they overthrow the established authority in society. Of course, then their task is to establish a new social structure with new positions regarded as legitimate. Their task is to make charismatic authority into traditional or legal-rational authority.

Weber's analysis is very insightful. It reminds us how important position in organization is as a power resource. We can apply his points to virtually every social relationship. Over time, we develop a structure that we come to accept. Acceptance of the structure is the acceptance of its inequality of positions; it is, over time, the acceptance of authority, legitimate power.

There is more to position than legitimacy, however. Let us look further.

THE INEVITABILITY OF INEQUALITY
IN ORGANIZATION

Most of us believe in democracy. We believe that the people should somehow rule themselves. The concepts of "social structure" and "authority" seem to contradict the possibility of democracy, to some extent, since both concepts emphasize inequality of power.

No one makes this point better than Robert Michels (1876–1936), who developed an important sociological theory which has come to be called *the iron law of oligarchy* (1915). Oligarchy means the "rule of a few," and Michels's law translates into the idea that wherever organization exists there will be a few people who dominate. This is not because we are evil or weak or stupid; it is, instead, because organization itself releases strong tendencies for this to occur.

It all begins with leaders. Wherever leaders are chosen to coordinate the activities of any group, formal organization, community, or society, then oligarchy begins. Michels did not emphasize legitimacy as Weber did. Instead, he pointed out that position is a tremendously important resource in other ways. With it comes access to information, control over what others below are told, greater knowledge of the working of organization, and an alliance with others in high positions. Those in high positions come to believe that the organization "is theirs," that they know what is good, so they increasingly act to protect themselves, and much of what they do is designed to keep themselves in power. Those below give up control of the organization: They do not know what is going on so they must trust others above them, they tend to be disorganized, and, after all, they have other things to do than to question others "who are in a position to know." It becomes very difficult to challenge decisions that have already been made by those in high position.

Michels seems to hit on some very important insights which describe the nature of American society today in both our political system and in the formal organizations of which we all find ourselves a part of. The gulf between leaders and others is very great: High positions give advantages which are not very easily overcome. Note how decisions are made in fraternities, student senates, church boards, and other voluntary organizations. In most cases a few make the decisions; the rest, for reasons Michels makes clear, have little choice but to accept.

Both Michels and Weber underline the importance of positions for bringing power to actors in social organization. Weber focuses on the strength of legitimacy; Michels focuses on the strength of the leadership position itself.

CLASS POSITION AND POWER

Social power was very important to Karl Marx also. Marx believed that real power came from ownership: ownership of the means of production in society. If one owned the means of production (factories, large businesses, large farms, banks), then one possessed a great resource. One had great power in relation to others. He called such people "the ruling class."

Whereas Weber and Michels emphasized the importance of positions in organization as sources of power, Marx emphasized class, *economic position*. If one was part of the ruling class, then one had control over other people's jobs, and this gave great control over other people's lives. The ruling class in society, because of the great importance of their economic power, are also able to control government, the law and courts, education, the military, and all other important aspects of society. The ruling class is also able to control the dominant ideas, values, and norms in society. That is because they have the resources necessary to perpetuate their ideas, values, and norms. Control over property gives one greater control over culture too.

Weber too saw the importance of class in determining power in society. Weber's definition of class was broader than Marx's. A class to Weber was simply one's economic rank in society based on a whole number of criteria: income, wealth, ownership of wealth producing property, and so on. Economic rank—class—meant the ability of an individual to achieve his or her will in the economic arena. Thus, class to Weber was "economic power." And Weber, like Marx, saw that economic power often could influence power in government and in other human relationships. Thus, in addition to his emphasis on authority in organization Weber emphasized economic power too as a power resource.

Both Marx and Weber are emphasizing what most of us have come to accept in our common-sense notion of reality. "Money is power": Wealth, in the form of control over the means of production (in the case of Marx), or in many forms (as in the case of Weber), brings the individual or group the ability to win in relation to others. It means that one is better able to direct society to meet his or her own interests; it means that society is built to conform to one's own interests rather than others. It means that in interaction with others, one is more likely to get his or her way; it also means that it is difficult for others to control one's life (independence).

Poverty is at the other end of the spectrum. Marx described the worker in a very dependent position. Nothing is more important than economic survival. If one is dependent on someone else for this, then the other has control over his or her life. If I work for someone else, if my job depends on him or her, then my life is not my own. This is the heart of Marx's thinking about power and powerlessness. Workers are exploited: They work for other people who get rich off of their labor. They are paid little so that the employers can grow rich. This is the heart of a class society.

To both Marx and Weber, poverty is powerlessness. It is a position of dependence on others for survival, for work, for food and shelter. Spending time surviving allows little time for influencing society. Poverty brings no power resources: One has no money and no position in society. Generally, poor people lack organization and leaders trying to bring about change, since the business of poverty is survival.

To a great extent, then, it makes good sense to think of class as *power*. Class position brings people resources or lack of them. So long as a society is a class society, there will be an *inequality of power*. Describing society simply as a democracy is to overlook this important fact.

ORGANIZATION AS POWER

Robert Michels believed that the masses in organization were really incapable of organizing themselves and significantly controlling organization. Both Marx and Weber argued that organization was a very important power resource.

Indeed, for Marx this was the workers' only real resource against the power of the ruling class. Someday, Marx believed, workers would come together, communicate, and share a consciousness of class position—a realization that society is organized by and for a few people in the ruling class and that the rest are simply controlled and exploited. Eventually this will bring organization, conflict, and, eventually, revolution.

Weber too saw the central importance of organization. Indeed, Weber believed that organization is a third source of power in society (besides authority and class). Everywhere people organize themselves. Some organizations are made up of and represent upper-class people: business associations, private clubs, and political pressure groups. There are also middle-class and working-class organizations: unions, professional associations, and so on. There are also in society organizations of people who share interests other than class interests: black, Jewish, Hispanic, Catholic, and Protestant organizations, women's organizations, and fraternal organizations. Doctors, lawyers, teachers, and plumbers form organizations, as do those who oppose or defend the right to own guns or have an abortion. All of these organizations mean power in society. Alone, the individual can do little, but together people can organize themselves, pool their resources, and affect society. Of course, all such groups are not equal. Effectiveness depends on leadership, commitment, careful organization, money, numbers, and knowledge.

SUMMARY

We have here tried to show that social power arises from various sources, not just one.

1. Power arises from authority. Authority means that one fills a position in organization that others regard as legitimate. One has a recognized "right to command." Such authority may arise from tradition, the law, or from a belief by people that one has extraordinary personal qualities.
2. Power arises from positions of leadership in organization. Positions of leadership bring extraordinary opportunities to control people in organization and to direct the organization.
3. Power arises from wealth. It arises from class position in society. Poverty brings powerlessness.
4. Power arises from organization itself. People who are organized well have greater opportunity to achieve their will than those who are not organized.

Modern theories of social power are built on these ideas. There are three basic theories, and each one sees a different system of power in American society. Each points to a different source of power. These three theories are called:

1.   *Pluralism:* Power is distributed among many organizations in society.
2.   *The power elite:* Power is in the hands of a few people who fill certain key positions in society.
3.   *The corporate elite:* Power is in the hands of a few who control the modern corporation.

PLURALISM

Of the three theories, pluralism is the only theory which describes power diffused throughout most of society. It is a theory consistent with what many people believe about power in the United States. It is a theory which does not focus on inequality of class and inequality of position; instead, it focuses on organizations of people as the most important source of power in American life.

Pluralism is actually a theory of democracy. How can millions of people rule themselves? How can we get everyone involved? How can we check our rulers? How can we check those who have wealth and position? How can we fight the inequality that exists in society so that everyone participates? The answer that the pluralist gives is always in the fact that *power arises from organizations of people.*

In the nineteenth century, Alexis de Tocqueville described Americans as joiners. We join together to get our way. We join together to make sure that our interests are being met. We join together to get rid of political leaders we dislike, and we join together to make sure that laws we believe in are passed. It is through organization—political parties, religious organizations, pressure groups, occupational and business associations—that people are able to effectively participate in government. Such participation means that a few leaders will not rule (as Michels feared), that the upper class will not control us (as Marx thought), and that authority will not command without question (as Weber predicted). To the pluralist, power rests in the people through their organizations.

Democracy is conflict within rules. It is disagreement over ideas and interests. It is competition for power. Because there are so many groups, and because we each belong to several, in the end all of us are represented, and over time, the interests of everyone are met, at least to some extent. When some people are not represented, they get together and form another organization.

There is no illusion here that democracy is the power of the individual. Few social scientists accept this notion. Instead, power is said to belong to groups struggling to get their interests met. There is no belief here that those who fill positions in government have the real power; real power lies in the competing organizations, which represent the people and influence those in political positions.

This first model of power may be correct to some extent. Clearly, organizations of people play a role in influencing government. However, most sociologists are critical of this theory precisely because it overlooks too much the concepts emphasized throughout this book (and throughout the sociological perspective): social structure, social class, and social power. Most argue that some version of an elite theory of power better explains American society and most other societies.

THE POWER ELITE

The Power Elite (1956), by C. Wright Mills, an important American sociologist, was a landmark book, for it took issue with pluralism and documented the dominance of a power elite in the United States.

Mills is very sociological in his approach. The United States is dominated by a few people who fill positions in three sectors: the economy, the military, and the government. Specifically, the United States is run by a few corporate executives, the top officers in the military, and the few who control the executive branch of government. These constitute three elites in society.

On the one hand, these elites compete for power. In the post–Civil War period, the economic elite dominated the United States. With the depression in the 1930s, the political elite rose to the top, and after World War II the military elite took over.

On the other hand, the three elites are one. Mills tries very hard to show us that these elites intermarry, come from the same families, go to the same schools, interact, and know each other well. He shows that corporate boards are filled with retired generals, political leaders come from corporate boards, and generals come from rich families.

And Mills describes the masses in a similar way as Michels: disorganized, apathetic, without knowledge, and trusting.

Mills has many critics, but his influence has been great. Most believe that he exaggerated the power of the military, but many sociologists see a wisdom in his general view: an attempt to take power seriously, to uncover the important positions in society, and to show who fills them and with what result. There is also an element of Marx here: The power elite rules primarily in its own interests, and it influences everything that we do and all that we believe and value.

THE CORPORATE ELITE

There are those who have built on Mills. For example, C. William Domhoff (1967) has identified the power elite in seven sectors in society, dominated by an upper social class of families with great wealth. There are those who try to fight the ideas of Mills, who study power along pluralist lines. There are also those, such as Suzanne Keller, who accept the idea that modern society is dominated by an elite, but believe that the elite is really several elites, competing for dominance, each checking one another, each representing different interests in society, almost acting like a pluralism among the elites.

However, probably the most important group influenced by Mills are those who have concentrated their attention on certain positions in society: the top positions in the modern corporation. Money is not the most important resource. Neither is political or military position, or even class position. Organizations do not rule society either. The most important resources in modern society are a few positions in the corporation, belonging to the executives and the boards of directors. To fill these positions is to have a resource that allows for great influence in society and in the world.

The modern corporation controls huge amounts of wealth. It employs large numbers of people, produces the goods in society, and controls much of the money. Corporations pay for the advertising and thus influence our wants, our ideas, and our values. They influence the kind of work we all do, and they influence the nature of our education. Their activities influence which area of the country is prosperous and which is poor, and thus they even influence where we all live. They influence every aspect of American life.

The success of corporations depends on what the government and military do. Their success depends on a foreign policy that guarantees friendly foreign governments, a military policy that encourages the production of military goods, and a tax policy that encourages corporate growth. Many are multinational and thus their success depends on a world order that guarantees markets for their products and a stable source of labor and raw materials. It is therefore essential that political and military leaders are influenced as much as possible.

As most Americans have come to realize, small business is dying, increasingly taken over by larger and larger corporations. This increases dramatically the power of the corporation and those who control the top positions there. In 1980, for example, the top 0.1 percent of all corporations (2,900 firms) owned 70 percent of all the assets of all American corporations. (U.S. Bureau of the Census, *Statistical Abstract,* 1984, 540, 546)

Who controls the corporation, and who is it that influences our lives? The answer, according to many researchers who have spent a great deal of time and effort investigating the matter, is a very few individuals who are united in a number of ways with one another, and who have close relationships with political leaders in society. Corporate leaders—executives and boards of directors—do not simply fill positions in one corporation. They are often involved in several. In a study of 123 corporations done by the U.S. Senate Committee on Governmental Affairs, it was found that in 1978, the thirteen largest of these corporations had overlapping memberships with 70 percent of the other corporations. A truly corporate elite— united in interests, in outlook, and in power—has emerged:

> The unplanned consequence, however, is the formation of a communications network that defines an inner circle of the business community in each country that can rise above the competitive atomization of the many corporations that constitute its base and concern itself with the broader issues affecting the entire large-firm community. (Useem, 1984, 57)

Society is, therefore, increasingly controlled by a small economic elite, an elite that fills the top positions in a few corporations and influences more and more the lives of all of us in society and indeed societies all over the world. Power is highly concentrated, according to this theory of power, and real democracy is a fiction.

SUMMARY

Each theory of power summarized here is important to understand, if we are to understand the nature of American society. We are a society of organizations, each working in its own interests and trying to affect the direction of society. We are a society of political, economic, and military elites, each with a power base, and to some extent united into a single elite. We are a society of corporations, each with great amounts of power, together dominated by an elite, united to some extent.

We should not forget that the United States is also a class society, and that in our everyday lives, the upper class is more powerful than the rest of us, and that the poor have almost no power in relation to the rest of us.

The introduction of the concept "power" into our analysis of interaction and social organization is critical for understanding human beings. Power is a central part of social structure and social class. Those who have power shape the culture and institutions that make up society. Those who have power have the most to gain by social order, and it is they, more than anyone, who develop the instruments of social control. The study of all interaction and all social organization must, in the end, take into account power: potential power, actual power, and the exertion of power. We are not all equals. Some influence and some are influenced; some control and some are controlled. Remember always the importance of resources in social life.

QUESTIONS TO CONSIDER

1. What is the meaning of social power? In describing this, be sure to also describe the meaning of potential power, actual power, exertion of power, resources, influence, control, and powerlessness.
2. Think of a dyad or group you are part of. Identify the individual(s) with the most power. What are the resources that make them powerful?
3. Positions bring power to those who fill them. Take an example of a position: president of the United States, president of your university, president of a corporation. Describe—using both Weber and Michels—the many ways that one can use position to achieve his or her will.

4. What are the most powerful organizations in this society? Try to identify the resources they have; try to identify the interests they work for.

5. What is pluralism? To what extent does pluralism describe the nature of American society?

RECOMMENDED READING

BLAU, PETER M. 1964. *Exchange and power in social life.* New York: Wiley.
DOMHOFF, G. WILLIAM. 1967. *Who rules America?* Englewood Cliffs, N.J.: Prentice-Hall.
DOMHOFF, G. WILLIAM. 1983. *Who rules America now? A view for the 80s.* Englewood Cliffs, N.J.: Prentice-Hall.
EMERSON, RICHARD. 1962. Power-Dependence Relations. *American Sociological Review* 27: 31–41.
GAMSON, WILLIAM. 1968. *Power and discontent.* Homewood, Ill.: Dorsey Press.
HAWLEY, AMOS H. 1963. Community power and urban renewal success. *American Journal of Sociology* 68: 422–431.
HUNTER, FLOYD. 1953. *Community power structure.* Chapel Hill, N.C.: University of North Carolina Press.
LIPSET, SEYMOUR M., MARTIN TROW, and JAMES COLEMAN. 1956. *Union democracy.* New York: Free Press.
MICHELS, ROBERT. 1915. *Political parties.* 1962 ed. Trans. Eden and Cedar Paul. New York: Free Press.
MILLS, C. WRIGHT. 1956. *The power elite.* New York: Oxford University Press.
OLSEN, MARVIN E. 1978. *The process of social organization.* New York: Holt, Rinehart, and Winston.
RUSSELL, BERTRAND. 1938. *Power.* New York: W. W. Norton and Company.
TOCQUEVILLE, ALEXIS DE. [1835] 1945. *Democracy in America.* New York: Vintage Books.
U.S. BUREAU OF THE CENSUS. 1984. *Statistical abstract of the United States.* Washington, D.C.: U.S. Government Printing Office.
USEEM, MICHAEL. 1984. *The inner circle.* New York: Oxford University Press.
WEBER, MAX. [1924, 1964]. The theory of social and economic organization. Ed. A.M. Henderson and Talcott Parsons. Glencoe, Ill.: Free Press.
WRONG, DENNIS. 1980. *Power, its forms, bases and uses.* New York: Harper and Row.

The Japanese Robe by Alfred Stevens, Belgian (1828–1906). Oil on canvas. 36 ½ x 25 ⅛ inches. The Metropolitan Museum of Art, New York. Bequest of Catharine Lorillard Wolfe, 1887. Catharine Lorillard Wolfe Collection. (87.15.56) Reprinted with permission.

11

Symbols, Self, and Mind: Our Active Nature

Sometimes sociologists get too involved in describing the human being as a totally shaped organism. In ways it comes with the territory, since the real purpose of sociology (as well as all other sciences) is to understand *what causes* something—what causes human action. The question does not lend itself to an investigation of freedom or individuality.

Almost every sociologist believes that the human organism is to some extent an individual and to some extent free. Much of our work, however, has documented social patterns, socialization, and social control, leading students to wonder how individuality and freedom are possible in a sociological perspective.

We will now turn our attention to this question. In doing so, much will be borrowed from the social theory of George Herbert Mead (1863–1931), whose work—especially *Mind, Self and Society* (1934)—has had a great impact on sociology and offers a good introduction to the human being as an "active" organism.

INDIVIDUALITY AND FREEDOM

Perhaps the most important questions thinking people ask concern the relationship between the individual and society: Are we simply the product of our social life? Do we make free choices? Do we have any impact over the direction of society? Is there any real individuality?

Many of us go through college and the rest of our lives without seriously considering such questions. "Of course, I am an individual." "Of course, I am free." Such assertions are part of our taken-for-granted reality; they are embedded in the culture of the United States. Indeed, we say we enjoy living in this society because we are free and we are allowed to be individuals. The problem is far more complex than this, however—as the first ten chapters make clear: How free are we, and how much individuality can we really claim, given the power of social structure, culture, socialization, social controls, and the feelings of loyalty to organization we have?

If we scrape the surface of our own philosophies of life we will see that ideas about freedom are central to our views on a number of matters. Most of us assume freedom when we argue that individuals will be judged by God in the *choices* made in life: good or evil, faith or nonfaith, truth or falsehood. Our attitudes toward poverty, crime, and punishment are based on our ideas concerning the individual's ability to exercise choice. When other people act, we may hold them responsible for what they do or we may say, "They have no choice!" It is always interesting to notice how many of us will fall into the trap of blaming the individual who does things we disapprove of and then talk about a good home, luck, opportunities associated with social class, or religious training as being responsible if the individual does something we like.

A philosophy of freedom is central to our political ideas. The 1960s were a cry to extend freedom to blacks, and the 1970s to women. Presidents Kennedy and Johnson tried to fight poverty to extend freedom to the poor. We were told that the Vietnam War was fought for freedom; we were also told that it must be stopped in the name of freedom. Presidents Reagan and Bush ran for office in the name of economic freedom, and much of Reagan's foreign policy was defended as the last great hope for political freedom in the world. Groups cry out for freedom of choice, freedom of speech, freedom to worship, and freedom of the press. To many in the United States, communism means the end to freedom; to others, there is little freedom in a world where corporations dominate much of what people do.

Individualism is also central to U.S. culture. The pioneer, the farmer, the immigrant who makes it big, and the poor man who becomes president are our heroes. The appeal of rock music is in part the worship of the individual, and the respect we have for powerful people in history leads back to this value.

Not all societies value freedom and individualism. In some, commitment to kin is far more important. In some, commitment to tradition, God, or society itself overshadows freedom or individuality. That is why, perhaps, social science may not be welcome in the West, for, after all, social science questions what most of us accept— the reality of individuality and freedom.

It is important to separate freedom from individuality. Freedom means that *the actor actively makes choices and directs self in situations. The actor is in control.* This may mean the actor is an individual; it may also mean the actor is like other individuals. I may, after all, actively choose to conform. Individuality means that *the actor is unique: The actor is different from others around him or her.* This may mean freedom; it may also mean that the actor is not free, but is controlled by various internal or external forces (for example, by his or her unconscious and/or by organization). For example, I may fly off the handle all the time, making me an individual around those who are able to control themselves, but not making me very free. Or I may be shaped and controlled by a religious group which is very unique and which makes me very different from everyone else in my neighborhood.

Freedom has to do with *cause.* In earlier chapters we placed cause outside the individual in social organization. But if freedom exists, it exists when the individual is his or her own cause, exercising control over self and situation. No such freedom can be complete—it is always limited—since choice and control always exist in the context of social forces.

Individuality has to do with *differences.* No matter where we look in the world, even in the most totalitarian societies, we can find some individuality in all people, some differences among them. How significant these differences appear depends on who is investigating. Students in a college classroom may claim they vary greatly, and indeed they do if we focus on some qualities, such as interests, politics, talents, and plans. Yet if we take a broader perspective— such as that of an investigator from the Soviet Union—the differences will tend to disappear. What looks like difference to the people involved becomes sameness to an outsider, especially one from another society. From a broad perspective, Americans are the same; on closer inspection, we are all different.

HOW CAN WE EXPLAIN INDIVIDUALITY?

In part, individuality is like all other human qualities: It arises in interaction with others. We are all different—and some of us are very different—partly because we each have a unique set of interactions, positions, cultures, and socialization experiences. We are all subject to a different set of social controls. Each actor faces a different set of influences, each is the convergence of a different set of social forces. Even people in the same family will be different: Each sibling is in a different position in the family structure and is influenced by a different set of siblings ("You are my brother; I am your brother—we each have different brothers"). People who are in the same family will still have gender differences, differences in generation, and all will have different friends, teachers, and adults with whom they interact. Societies—or families—cannot create identical actors precisely because each actor has a different set of social organizations and a different history of interaction. And interaction can never be fully controlled or predetermined.

We are all different in part because of biological differences. Boys and girls are different in some aspects of their physical appearance and in some aspects of hormonal balance. We may have different temperaments, potentials, and appearance. Each of these helps make us unique. More important, however, how others around us react to such qualities will compound these differences.

We are also individuals because each of us has at least some control over our own choices. We are free to some extent. Not only does society control and shape us, but we, in turn, take control from society and shape our own lives. Whatever is told us is shaped into our own unique ideas. Whatever we are told to do is to some extent considered and often altered by us.

We are individuals, then, because (a) each of us has a different interaction history and is subject to a slightly different set of social forces; (b) each of us is biologically different, and this influences others' reactions to us; and (c) each of us is a free actor, at least to some extent.

But how can we account for freedom? Are we born with this quality? Is it part of our "nature"? Is it, like individuality, traceable to our social life?

THE ORIGIN OF HUMAN FREEDOM

George Herbert Mead and those sociologists who share his views believe that *freedom, like everything else about us, comes from our social life.* Humans are social to their very core, and we are not only imprisoned by this fact but also set free by it. It is responsible for our ability to break out, to control our self, to act back on society, and to direct our self away from what the socializers and controllers want. To understand this, we must understand that other people, by socializing us to become what they want, provide us with tools to independently decide what we want.

Socialization, then, is not simply the process by which the individual learns social organization—its patterns and controls—but also the process by which the individual develops qualities that make freedom possible. More specifically, it is through socialization that the individual takes on three important qualities: *symbols, self, and mind.* These, in turn, are qualities necessary for human freedom.

To understand them better, let us now turn our attention to one at a time.

THE MEANING AND IMPORTANCE OF SYMBOLS

Human beings, totally helpless at birth, without instinct to guide them, must rely on other people—on socialization—to show the way to deal with situations. This is accomplished through the child imitating the adult, through rewards and punishments given by the adult, but most of all through the words used by the adult to identify the world, the person, the rules, the patterns, and so on. Even an action—any kind of punishment, for example—usually includes a set of words that identify the type of behavior isolated as wrong ("Don't pick those flowers!" or "Don't ever pick any flowers!" or "Don't ever pick flowers that have not bloomed!" or "Don't ever pick flowers that belong to someone else!" or "Don't ever pick flowers without asking me first!"). A category of reality is labeled; we are taught how we are supposed to act in relation to that category of reality.

But unlike other animals, which can be trained to respond to words, the child learns how to *use* words. Our socializers are symbol users; we then take on these symbols and they become ours to use. This transforms us into beings who can *think*, to *choose*, to *control self*, and ultimately to break off from the controls of the socializers. *Socialization, because it depends so much on symbols, ends up leading to actions unplanned by the socializers.*

Most of us do not appreciate the importance of symbols to what we are. Humans use symbols when they communicate, socialization depends on symbols, as does cooperation, thinking, and problem solving.

Words are symbols, but objects may be symbols too, such as a flower or ring which may mean friendship or love. Many of our acts are also symbols. When I shake my fist I am telling you I feel angry, and when I throw my arms around you I am telling you something about my feelings about seeing you. Raising your hand in class tells me you want to say something, stamping out of the room in the middle of the lecture tells me you are upset, and putting your coat on tells me you are ready to leave.

Symbols are words, acts, and objects used to communicate and represent. Communication can be among people or within the individual. We give other people messages; we also converse with ourselves.

Communication can occur among animals without symbols. That is because acts—sounds or movements—can be cues that other animals respond to. In a sense non–symbol users turn each other on. Symbols, however, are "meaningful" acts. That is to say, symbols *represent* something to the actor. The actor understands that "x" represents number 1, "wine" represents a supernatural being, the word "elephant" represents a type of animal characterized by a long trunk, and a "kiss" represents a romantic attachment. To say that a symbol represents something is to say that the user of the symbol (the speaker, writer, actor, and so on) *understands* his or her own acts. Not only does a symbol user give off cues to others, but the message given off is understood by the actor communicating. This quality of symbols—what George Herbert Mead called "meaningful"—makes communication possibilities infinitely greater, complex ideas possible, and thinking (talking to oneself) a central characteristic of the symbol user.

Symbols in Mead's interpretation are something *used intentionally* by the actor to communicate. I talk to you on purpose, I share my thoughts or intentions with you on purpose. Symbolic communication, unlike other forms of communication, is understood by the person communicating to another. It is, to some extent, an act controlled by the actor.

Of course, part of human communication is not truly symbolic. We communicate without realizing it; we give off body language that others respond to or even interpret. To say that humans are symbol users much of the time is not to deny all these other ways we communicate, but to isolate one very important human quality and examine its usefulness.

How is meaning established? How do we come to understand what something represents? The answer is apparent: Symbols are created among people in interaction. They are social, not instinctive. They are assigned meaning through agreement; meaning is not fixed in nature. We can make any word, act, or object into a symbol. A rock is not usually thought to be a symbol, but you and I can determine that a certain rock in a certain place will represent danger. I can show off my horse, and my horse becomes a symbol of my wealth, my skill, or my values. Words are almost always symbols. Giving you the peace sign is a symbol and crossing my arms can be a symbol if we so decide. Symbols are shared among people, and whatever people decide should be a symbol becomes one.

Of course, using symbols does not always work smoothly. Sometimes I use symbols to communicate but no one listens. Or sometimes I do not mean to communicate but others will interpret my acts as symbolic. Or I can mean one thing by my symbols but others think I mean something else. Symbols are almost never perfectly shared, and there is often the possibility for misunderstanding. For a "perfect" symbol to exist, it would have to be perceived and understood by others in exactly the same way that it was intended by the user.

There are two ways that symbols play a central role in our lives:

1. *Human social organization depends on symbols.* Most other animal societies are based either on instinct or imitation; they do not have the complexity and flexibility that symbolic behavior permits.

Human society demands lifelong socialization, and human socialization uses symbols. All that is cultural—values, goals, norms, and truths—is symbolic. All accumulation of knowledge which is passed from one generation to the next is dependent on socialization through symbols.

Further, social organization demands that human beings communicate with each other as they cooperate, as problems are encountered and worked out. Symbolic communication is central to group problem solving.

2. *The human individual depends on symbols.* Symbols are what we use to communicate with ourselves; that is, most of our thinking consists of symbol use. It is through word symbols that we analyze situations, define them, apply our past experiences, and predict the consequences of our action. Symbol use means we are problem solvers in our world; we plan our action, rather than just respond to stimuli. Symbols also allow us to catalogue experience, to store it all in a tremendously complicated memory bank, to organize a mass of meaningful details which become available to us for application in particular situations. While we act we are not limited to the present physical situation. We can think of the past and future, and we can consider things we never encountered directly, like Russia or heaven or going to the moon. Finally, symbols open up to consideration an abstract world, a world which is only symbolic, a world which does not exist in our physical environment. We can consider things like freedom, love, God—and most of the concepts of a perspective like sociology. And we can create new, fictional worlds by actively manipulating symbols into different combinations.

So symbols are the basis for human thinking, and thinking in turn is basic to what we do in situations. We do not just respond to the world presented to us by others; we manipulate that world in our heads with the use of symbols, and we act accordingly. We do not just fill status positions. We also think about them, we define our roles in them, make decisions on how to act, and even change them as we go along. Sometimes we may conform without much thinking, but almost always there is some analysis on our part, some decision making. Teachers fill status positions and conform to expectations of students, but they also will critically evaluate those expectations. Sometimes teachers worry about what student expectations appear to be, and they think about how to make their teaching better and even how to try to influence student expectations. Students, too, do more than simply fill status positions. They evaluate, plan, try shortcuts, play around with the situations they encounter, and when trouble arises they think of ways to deal with it.

The interesting thing about word symbols is that the individual is able to manipulate them creatively, to arrive at unique solutions to problems, to develop new ideas, term papers, books, and artistic products. Indeed, there is some creativity in everything we do. The situations we encounter every day are not identical to earlier situations, so we must adjust ourselves ever so slightly, apply what we know, and work out our action. Each person we meet and every problem we confront demands that we think out our actions ourselves rather than depending entirely on what we have learned from others. It is through the internal manipulation of symbols that humans become creative, active, choosing individuals.

Rather than requiring robots, human social organization demands *thinking* actors, and part of the "problem" with thinking actors is that they are difficult to control completely, so actors within all social organization end up questioning, criticizing, challenging, and shaping the direction of social organization. Symbols, then, as well as the capabilities they make possible in the human being, make us all into free actors, at least to some extent.

WE POSSESS SELF AND MIND

Along with symbols, self and mind are also important qualities that make possible a more active, free being.

What is a self? Is it our true essence? Is it the same as our personality? Is it a little person within us waiting to be encouraged to grow and unfold?

For most sociologists the self simply means *the person as object,* an object that the actor can look back on and act back on. We all act toward our environment, toward other people and objects, but we also are able to act back toward our self. We can talk to our self. We can look at our self and judge ourselves as good or bad, nice or not nice, beautiful or ugly, wise or stupid. We can look at our self in relation to others and assess how people are acting toward us; we can assess the effects of their acts on us, and our acts on them. We are also able to call our self a name—to give ourselves an identity (man, American, boss). We direct our self; that is, we exercise self-control. We tell ourselves how to act. This constant conversation with our self is a big part of the reason we end up acting as we do.

What is the significance of selfhood? Let us try to be a little more systematic:

1. The conversation we all carry on with the self is called *thinking.* Thinking is the actor pointing things out to himself or herself, figuring out situations, problem solving, analyzing what others are doing, assessing what he or she is doing in relation to others. Thinking—talking to self with symbols—allows us to make decisions in situations, to control what we do in situations.

2. Selfhood means we are able to talk to self *about self.* We see ourselves in situations; we are *self-aware.* We are aware of ourselves as objects in the environment that others act toward and that we as actors act toward. We realize that we are affected by others and that we have an effect. We can *assess* how we do. We can judge our self, liking or disliking what we do and what we are. Over time, we develop a *self-concept.* And we call ourselves names—that is, we establish *identities,* and we tell others who we think we are.

3. To possess a self also means that we can exercise *self-direction* in situations. Instead of simply being pushed around by our environment—conditioned or manipulated by it—we are instead able to turn back on our self, think and see ourselves in the situation, and *tell ourselves how to act* in the situation. We are in control to some extent, holding back action, planning action, trying out plans, evaluating and reevaluating our efforts. Sometimes we do this very

consciously and deliberately; most of the time we do this very quickly and we are barely conscious of what we are doing.

Selfhood thus makes each of us a being in conversation with self, conscious of self, and in control of our self. It means that we are able to temper the influence of others on what we do. It does not mean that others are not important; it means only that in addition to their influence, the actor is able to interpret, add to, plan, and assess, and, to some extent, control the situation.

But Mead makes the important point that the self, like symbols, is created by others in interaction with the individual. We come to see ourselves only by first seeing it through the acts and words of others. Others are the looking glass through which we become aware that we exist.

The self develops in stages. First we see others acting toward us, and we imitate their acts toward our self ("preparatory stage"). When we begin to take on language, we are able to understand the perspectives of "significant others" such as parents, and we take on these perspectives as our own and we talk to self as they do ("Nice boy." "You are intelligent." "You are Frank's brother." "Don't ask for a cookie until after dinner."). Mead calls this stage the "play stage," since the child uses the perspective of one person at a time to talk to self. Eventually we are able to assume the perspective of many people simultaneously, and thus develop a "generalized other," made up of all those who are important to us, and we converse with self and control self from that perspective. We have then become a member of society, since now we are able to assume the perspective and rules of society. This stage Mead calls the "game stage," since now we are able to understand the rules of a cooperative whole.

We are absolutely dependent on others for the development of our self; yet, as self develops we are able to take some control from others, we begin to hold private conversations, and we make choices in situations. The actor who has a mature self is able to take or leave what others say and do, interpret what is going on, and determine his or her own directions. We borrow the perspectives of others, but alter them to fit our needs to some extent; we use them as guides. We are able to tell ourselves to conform or to refuse conformity, to play a role as others expect or to test others out, to act creatively or to leave the social organization. *So the self, while grounded in society, allows for some individuality, some creative interpretation, some self-direction and choice.*

Mind is linked to self and symbols. It is easily confused with self and symbols. It arises in the human being at the same moment self and symbols arise. It is the third human quality that allows for some freedom.

Mind is thinking, all the conversation the actor carries on with the self. Mind is the actor talking to himself or herself. This activity involves all the ways the actor points things out to self. When we described above all the various ways the actor acts toward self, we were describing mind. *Mind is this action.*

Mind is not brain, nor is it all brain activity. It is, instead, a certain kind of brain activity, that activity we call thinking or talking to oneself. Mind action goes on all the time. We talk to ourselves from the moment we wake up until the moment we fall asleep at night. Thinking—mind action—becomes most obvious to us when we confront a new situation or when our action is interrupted and a problem must be overcome. Then our thinking becomes more conscious and deliberate; we must plan ahead. However, almost every situation demands some thinking as we act—quick, ongoing talking to self.

Symbols, self, and mind are easily confused since they are so intimately connected. Simply remember that symbols are things that the individual uses to communicate (including communicating with self), self is the object the individual communicates to (with symbols), and mind is all the action—with symbols—that we engage in toward the self.

SUMMARY

Mead's greatest insight is the idea that symbols, self, and mind, all interdependent and basic to our active nature, arise from society. These tools are not something we are born with, but something we develop only in interaction with others. That is why it is absolutely essential to understand that humans are *social* to their very core. Even our ability to act back, to say no, to control our self, to shape organization that is trying to shape us is a social creation. In truth, that which forms us gives us the necessary tools to form it. (See Figure 11-1)

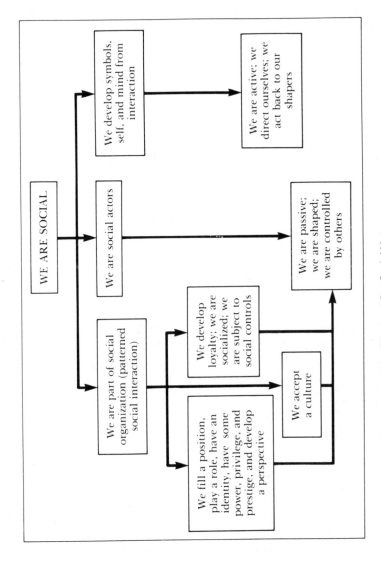

FIGURE 11–1 The Effects of Our Social Nature

QUESTIONS TO CONSIDER

1. This chapter argues that humans are to some extent free because of symbols, self, and mind. Can you explain this? Can you agree with it?
2. What are symbols? What is a self? What is mind? To what extent do the descriptions contained in this chapter differ from what you have learned elsewhere?
3. What is freedom? What is individuality? Are they different, as the chapter maintains?
4. Once again there is an attempt to tie what the human being is to society. Explain the links, according to this chapter.

RECOMMENDED READING

The following works examine the human as an active being. There is focus on symbols, self, mind, and socialization. They tend to be written from a symbolic interactionist perspective.

BECKER, ERNEST. 1962. *The birth and death of meaning.* New York: Free Press.

BERGER, PETER L., and THOMAS LUCKMANN. 1966. *The social construction of reality.* Garden City, N.Y.: Doubleday.

BLUMER, HERBERT. 1969. *Symbolic interactionism.* Englewood Cliffs, N.J.: Prentice-Hall.

BRIM, ORVILLE G., JR., and STANTON WHEELER. 1966. *Socialization after childhood: Two essays.* New York: Wiley.

CHARON, JOEL. 1989. *Symbolic interactionism.* 3rd ed. Englewood Cliffs, N.J.: Prentice-Hall.

COOLEY, CHARLES HORTON. [1902] 1964. *Human nature and the social order.* New York: Schoken Books.

DENZIN, NORMAN. 1972. The genesis of self in early childhood. *The Sociological Quarterly* 13: 291–314.

ELKIN, FREDERICK, and GERALD HANDEL. 1978. *The child and society.* 3d ed. New York: Random House.

FINE, GARY ALAN. 1979. *Small groups and culture creation. American Sociological Review* 44: 733–745.

GOFFMAN, ERVING. 1959. *The presentation of self in everyday life.* Garden City, N.Y.: Doubleday/Anchor.

HERTZLER, JOYCE O. 1965. *A sociology of language.* New York: Random House.

LINDESMITH, ALFRED R., ANSELM L. STRAUSS, and NORMAN DENZIN. 1974. *Social psychology.* 4th ed. Hinsdale, Ill.: Dryden.

McCALL, GEORGE J., and J. L. SIMMONS. 1978. *Identities and interactions.* New York: Free Press.

MEAD, GEORGE HERBERT. 1934. *Mind, self and society.* Chicago: University of Chicago Press.

MELTZER, BERNARD N. 1972. *The social psychology of George Herbert Mead.* Kalamazoo, Mich.: Center for Sociological Research, Western Michigan University.

ROSE, PETER I., ed. 1979. *Socialization and the life cycle.* New York: St. Martin's Press.
SHIBUTANI, TAMOTSU. 1961. *Society and personality.* Englewood Cliffs, N.J.: Prentice-Hall.
STRAUSS, ANSELM. 1978. *Negotiations.* San Francisco: Jossey-Bass.
X, MALCOLM, and ALEX HALEY. 1964. *The autobiography of Malcolm X.* New York: Grove Press.

The Persistence of Memory (1931) by Salvador Dali. Oil on canvas
9 ½ x 13 inches. Collection, The Museum of Modern Art, New York.
Given anonymously. Reprinted with permission.

12

Social Change

INDIVIDUAL CHANGE AND SOCIAL CHANGE

Individuals change. They grow up, they change their directions, their ideas, their friends, their values. As they change roles they change, and as they change groups or communities they change. Every organization we enter means change since we are faced with new kinds of controls, structure, and culture.

All interaction means that we must alter what we do according to what others are doing. Their expectations matter to us, and we give them some consideration. As a result, our directions change, and we make new plans for our lives. In interaction we negotiate with others over our roles. We experience role conflict and we change. We think about our situations and our lives since we have symbols, mind, and self, and we decide to go in new ways.

The sociological view of the individual is that the individual continuously changes. Change basically occurs for two reasons: (1) The individual is a symbol-using, problem-solving, active being with self and mind, always thinking and making choices, which often take him or her in new directions. (2) The individual is a social being; as the social context changes, the individual will change. The individual may go into new organizations, the individual may assume new positions in organization, the organization itself may change, or society may change. Most of this book has focused on these ideas.

We have tried to link the individual to a social context; we have tried to show that both individual stability and change are linked to that social context.

However, up to now, we have not considered social change. Our emphasis has been on order and stability in organization. But social organization also changes. Change is easily as important a topic in organization as order and stability.

With all of the factors defending order in organization, how is change possible? What causes social change? This is a difficult question, which sociologists have only begun to understand and most others explain only in oversimplified terms. "Things don't really change—there is nothing new under the sun," cries the skeptic. "History repeats itself," says the pessimist. "Change is bad. Materialism and selfishness are weakening our moral fiber," preaches the minister. "The social order and social change is God's plan for us," teaches another. "Change is the responsibility of each individual," argues the moralist. "Economics, it's all economics—that's the source of all change," some try to prove, or "It is only through revolution that things change," cry the disgruntled.

Everyone seems to have a key to social change. Each of these may have something important to say, but each is far too simple. Social change and its causes is not a simple matter.

In fact, even defining what constitutes social change is not an easy matter. How much does something have to change to call it change? Has the relative position of blacks and whites changed since the Civil War? Yes and no, depending on one's definition of change.

We speak of change when we say something is significantly different today than it has been in the past. We speak of *social change* when *a social pattern (structure, culture, institutions) is significantly different today than it has been in the past.*

The question to be considered here is: What causes social patterns to change? There are many factors, and sociologists differ as to which is the most important. In this chapter we will summarize six:

1. Acts of people: individuals and organizations working for change
2. Social conflict
3. Outside influences: other organizations and the physical environment
4. Technology, including bureaucratization
5. Population changes

1. ACTS OF PEOPLE CHANGE SOCIAL ORGANIZATION

Social organization changes through the acts of social actors, communicating to, interpreting, and influencing one another. Each actor occasionally tries to have an impact on the social patterns, and some may be slightly successful. This is more true in dyads than it is in societies, and it is more true of small societies than of large ones. Since all human social organization is made up of active symbol-using beings with minds and selves, there are always actors who make attempts to test, to redefine the environment, to alter others, perhaps to deviate from or challenge social patterns.

Some actors have more impact than others. This is due to the amount of *power* one has in the social organization. In society those people at the top of the various stratification and political systems are able to influence the direction of change much more dramatically than those at the bottom. Indeed, one aspect of all status positions, you may recall, is power, the ability to get one's way in relation to others in social organization. It is difficult for Andrew, my son, to change things in our family (although he tries), because my wife and I have the powerful positions. The president of the university I am part of can change that organization more easily than I can and much more easily than any student can. In society the president of the United States can have considerable impact, and so can the head of General Motors or the chief justice of the Supreme Court, or the head of the State Department. The power of the owners of the big corporations in American society has been extensively documented. Corporate leaders influence foreign policy, even playing a significant role in revolutions, as seems to have been the case in the overthrow of Allende in Chile. Oil company chiefs have an important influence on this society's energy policies through control of resources.

But in spite of these examples of individual impact, the power of structure, culture, and social controls, embedded in the past, makes it very difficult to make substantial changes in social organization (except perhaps in the dyad or small group). We all want to believe that the individual makes a difference in organization, but when faced with the patterns of social organization, each of us has minimal power to direct and shape social organization the way we choose. We are all caught up in social organizations at every level, whose patterns have great stability. These patterns work against change, especially dramatic change.

The paradox is that those in the positions to bring about the most change are least likely to desire change; having made it to the top, they have the greatest investment in the organization. Their goals, values, and identities will be tied to it. It is easy to complain about the conservatism of the powerful in a social organization, but we too are transformed by our new status positions as we rise in the hierarchy. Thus the nature of social structure itself works against the ability of individuals to have great impact. Those with the most power are usually least willing to change the social organization; those at the bottom have the most to gain with change but are the least able.

It is also important to emphasize that those with power have more than their positions on their side. Social controls protect the powerful, and socialization from family to school to media teach all in society the importance of accepting the structure as it is. Those who attempt to protect society as it is will have law, police, government, religion, and all other "legitimate" social organizations and institutions on their side. Social change directed by others is made difficult to carry out.

Some individuals, however, do have impact. Napoleon, Jesus, Lenin, Mao, Hitler, Mohammed, and Martin Luther King come to mind. Max Weber (1922) called such individuals "charismatic authority." They are powerful because they attract a following who regard them as expressing an almost supernatural quality (as if chosen by history or God or gods). They are revolutionary: they arise *against* the traditional or legal order. They gain a following, and although they often fail to achieve their goals completely, they may have impact either through a revolution (as did Castro and Mao), or through influencing authorities (as in the case of Martin Luther King).

Still, it is easy to exaggerate the influence of the single person. Individual success always depends on more impersonal social forces, of which the individual is largely an instrument. Hitler came to power at a time of economic and social collapse; Napoleon's armies attacked a European order that was already in decay.

Individuals may have some impact on social organization, but organized groups are likely to have more impact. Most of us who are dissatisfied simply grumble and do little; sometimes we try to change something; occasionally we join with others. The NAACP, Mothers Against Drunk Driving, and the National Organization for Women are examples of formal organizations created to bring change in society, and they have been successful to some extent.

When large numbers of people work together in a loosely organized effort to change society, they constitute a *social movement:* the gay rights movement, the women's movement, the civil rights movement, the anti-Vietnam War movement. Such attempts to influence the direction of society are successful to the extent that individuals can pool their resources and exert power. Charismatic leadership helps considerably, but so does determination, organization, and material resources.

Formal organizations and social movements change society, but it is difficult and success is limited. It is similar to the impact of individuals. Social structure and culture tend to be highly stable. The greatest impact will come from those who have the greatest power in society; most often social movements and protest organizations have little power, and they are opposed by those who have social power and by groups organized to resist change. The change that does occur through organized efforts usually takes place within a context of more far-reaching and impersonal social forces, which encourage such change.

Sometimes social movements get widespread support and result in revolution, which means that a rapid and profound change in social patterns has taken place. Usually, what we call a revolution does not actually alter the old structure, culture, or institutions very much, and the people in positions of power are simply replaced by others. Most historians point out, for example, that the American Revolution was not really a revolution at all, but that the old structure and culture remained intact, that indeed the American Revolution can be best understood as a war fought to maintain the established society. Occasionally, as in the French Revolution in 1789, or the Russian Revolution of 1917, or the more recent Cuban or Chinese revolutions, there will be a major upheaval that has great impact. The old order is overthrown and a new society emerges. But this is rare, it is usually exaggerated in terms of its scope, and in most cases what is claimed to be a revolution turns out to be a minor change in the long run. After all, it is difficult to wipe out the old; it is tempting to return to the security offered by tradition.

The power of organization is great; it has arisen over time, it is protected by a number of forces, and people are socialized to be accepting actors. Individuals, organizations, and social movements may have impact, but there are other factors to consider, often more important.

2. SOCIAL CONFLICT CHANGES ORGANIZATION

Conflict (open struggle between actors) brings change to social organization. In part, we must understand change as resulting from efforts by individuals, organizations, and social movements to bring change in society being met by efforts by others to counter change. To work for change inevitably brings open conflict with those who have a stake in the social patterns. This conflict itself causes change: I act in my interests, you in yours; you struggle against me, I against you; usually the social world we exist in is never the same again.

Most sociologists emphasize the role of conflict in social change. Durkheim emphasized the role that deviance plays: Actions bring the reactions of society, and individuals or groups are labeled deviant and dealt with. However, unless they are controlled completely, they continue to act, and, over time, their acts become legitimate, or, at the very least, they change society's definitions.

Conflict between actors may mean a discussion of differences, argument, violence, a strike, mass imprisonment, or even attempted revolution. Society changes—through compromise, a major adjustment, or even by greater repression. If open conflict is feared by those in power positions, they may alter the social organization to a degree in order to prevent it; for example, a small amount of the valued things may be redistributed, such as income or economic opportunity.

Of course, for Karl Marx, social conflict is the real basis for significant social change. The rich get richer, and the poor poorer. Over time, the poor will realize that their interests are not being met, they will unite, and they will fight for their interests. The reactions by authorities and the wealthy will simply create greater conflict, until total revolutionary conflict will occur and a new society created.

Ralf Dahrendorf (1959:125) argues the typical sociological position: "All that is creativity, innovation, and development in the life of the individual, his group, and his society is due, to no small extent,

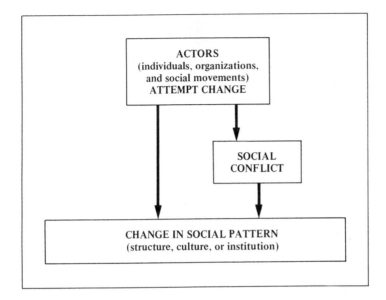

FIGURE 12–1 Actors, Conflict, and Social Change

to the operation of conflicts." Organization can never satisfy the needs and interests of everyone equally; there is always the potential for struggle over what it offers to its members (struggle over money, rights, power, prestige, who pays taxes, or who gets first choice of vacation time, or who is normal and who is deviant). So long as human differences exist there will be conflict; so long as there is conflict there will be change.

Two sources of change have been described thus far: actors attempting to change organization, and social conflict. Figure 12–1 summarizes what we have said here.

3. OUTSIDE FORCES CHANGE SOCIAL ORGANIZATION: THE SOCIAL AND PHYSICAL ENVIRONMENT

People travel to other societies. Sometimes they learn the new ways and settle there. Sometimes they bring armies and conquer other societies, forcing those other societies to become economically and politically dependent on the conquering society. In the continuous interaction that goes on between people from different societies, learning and sharing takes place. Societies change because other societies bring new ways.

When European nations conquered and explored most of the rest of the world in the eighteenth and nineteenth centuries, they brought with them their cultures and institutions. The subordinate societies changed, and much of the change was permanent. Even after colonial domination, these societies retained many of the ways of their former colonial masters. The old ways were no longer perceived as satisfactory.

The drive to industrialize and modernize has had a tremendous impact on most societies in the twentieth century. For the most part industrialization has been thrust on the world through Western expansion. Either because of the belief that industrialization and modernization is a good thing, because it is seen as a way to get rid of foreign domination, or because powerful interests in the society encourage it, most of the world, through contact with Western nations, has gone through tremendous structural, cultural, and institutional changes. Japan's history in the nineteenth and twentieth centuries is the most dramatic example of contact with outsiders, rapid industrialization, and dramatic social change. Yet Japan is also an example of a society that has been able to retain some core elements of its traditional culture. It is a blend of the old and new. It illustrates well the fact that social change does not occur the same way in all societies. Modernization occurs in the context of old social patterns.

It is not just society that changes because of outside social influences. A community (Dallas) or a formal organization (General Motors) changes because other communities and formal organizations change and have an impact through interaction. As industries get bigger, labor unions get bigger, and as labor unions get bigger, individual businesses must change in order to adjust. As one business changes, it causes competitors to change too. Japanese automobile companies influence American companies to change; as an automobile company changes in the United States, it is watched carefully and other companies adjust. As the companies change, the dealers change, and the unions, and all of these may affect Fran's Diner, which has tripled business as a result. A rebellion at Berkeley may affect all universities. A new kind of high school program in Minneapolis can be copied by high schools all over the country.

Thus, we should understand that social organizations are re-may affect all universities. A new kind of high school program in Minneapolis can be copied by high schools all over the country.

Thus, we should understand that social organizations are related to one another in many complex ways, and as one changes, it can affect others. Societies influence one another, as do communities, formal organizations, and groups.

Remember too that social organizations always exist within larger social organizations. As the larger ones change, they will cause smaller organizations to change. Changes in the world affect individual societies. As societies change, so will all social organizations within society, from dyad relationships to families to businesses and communities. As society builds schools to educate children, the family's culture is made less important: its norms, values, truths, and goals are changed, threatened, or rejected entirely. As structural changes take place in society and there are more opportunities for women in the corporate world, parents will be influenced to encourage female children to go in those directions. Changes in society filter down to changes in all social organization.

Not only does the outside social environment change social organization; the physical environment is also an important influence.

Structures, cultures, and institutions develop in response to the kinds of problems people face together. Some of these problems come from changes in the physical environment. Climatic changes may bring about a time of hardship in the farming community; small farmers go broke, and the large corporate farm wins out, since it has the resources to adjust to climatic changes. Climatic change may affect the occupational structure in society (fewer and fewer farmers), the political and class structure (less power in rural areas), and the prevailing societal institutions (the small family farm). The availability of large populations of wild animals has been central to hunting societies in Africa. What happens as these animals are destroyed by the pressure of increasing human population? The old ways will no longer be applicable to the changing physical environment. Earthquakes, tornadoes, and famines lead to change in communities, as does the slower process of environmental pollution.

A summary of the causes of social change we have considered thus far can be found in Figure 12–2.

Note one final point: The social and physical environment have two paths of influence. On the one hand, they directly influence

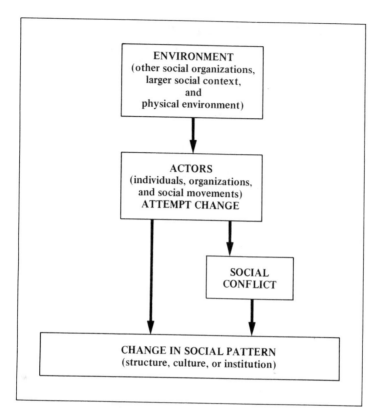

FIGURE 12–2   The Environment and Social Change

4. TECHNOLOGY CHANGES SOCIAL ORGANIZATION

Why do we act in the world the way we do? Max Weber pointed out that much of the way people do things can be divided into tradition and rationality. "We act the way we do because that is the way people like us have always acted." (tradition) "We act the way we do because it works for the problems we need to solve." (rationality) All societies are made up of both types of actions. After all, all societies must develop ways to feed themselves, and tradition determines part of it, but figuring out how to deal with new situations must take over now and then.

Weber described modern society as increasingly rational. There is an increasing tendency to escape traditional action and replace it with rational action: the application of knowledge to solving problems. This is the meaning of technology, and although there has been technology in every human society, modern life is thoroughly technological, and wherever new technology is introduced, change in society occurs.

Technology is the application of knowledge to the solution of practical problems. Machines are the most obvious examples of technology, but technology is also birth control devices, medicine, and developments in transportation and communication. Some sociologists consider technology to be the most important source of social change. It was the invention of the wheel, modern agricultural techniques, health-care breakthroughs, the automobile, and the telephone that significantly altered society, communities, formal organizations, groups, and dyads. Sociologists, William Ogburn and Meyer Nimkoff (1955), in a study which has influenced a great deal of thinking and research on the family, traced the following developments to the impact of technology: growing emphasis on romance, earlier marriages, smaller families, fewer functions for the family to perform in society, more wives working outside the home, more separation and divorce. A case study of a small town in 1951 documented how a seemingly minor technological change—switching from steam engines to diesel engines—literally wiped out a whole community whose existence was based on trains stopping there for water (Cottrell, 1951). It is fascinating to study how the automobile has affected everything in American life from travel to sexual behavior. And one only has to witness the impact of television in the last thirty years and the almost daily breakthroughs in computer technology to begin to appreciate the role of technology in American society.

People do not normally create technology in order to change society. Instead, they do it to solve a problem at hand. They do it to conquer a disease or put up a sturdier building. However, these developments together have profound effects on the nature of society, on its social structure, its culture, its institutions. The development of birth control devices, whatever their original purpose, has made a tremendous difference in a woman's ability to control her own life, and this, in turn, has had great effects on equality of men and women and the nature of the family. The mechanization of farming has dramatically changed the occupational structure of this society, has created a highly urbanized society, and has helped create American economic power in the world. Few people foresee very accurately the ultimate influence of their creations, and rarely do they create them in order to influence. However, whatever their purpose, the technology makes a great difference.

Bureaucracy is technology; it is social technology. Bureaucratic organization is a modern attempt to purposely create structures that can deal with the problems of a complex technological society. It is a calculated way of organizing people; it is an attempt to achieve goals efficiently and effectively. Like the machine, bureaucracy is an attempt to apply knowledge to a practical problem. "John, we have got to make our business work better. We can no longer rely on how we have always done things. They don't work. Let's streamline. Let's cut waste. Let's organize our business so that everyone knows exactly what to do. Let's not trust success to chance; let's try to assure it through careful thoughtful organization." This is the meaning of bureaucracy. The introduction of this view of organization to society has tremendous influence on the direction of society.

Max Weber (1922) wrote extensively on bureaucracy. A bureaucracy is an organization where the following principles are used:

1.   Positions are clearly and formally defined. Individuals know what they are supposed to do.

2.   There is a clearly laid-out power structure, organized in a hierarchy. People know who is responsible to whom.

3.   Rules are written down, and written records are kept of all activities. This helps assure organizational stability over time.

4.   Activities are impersonal. Feeling and tradition are minimized. Efficiency is the most important yardstick for determining what is done.

5.   Selection, evaluation, and promotion of people who fill positions are based on technical knowledge and performance, rather than friendship, family, or tradition.

Weber fully understood that no bureaucracy works exactly this way. In a sense, if bureaucracy worked as intended, these would be its qualities. He contrasted bureaucracy with earlier forms of organization (such as traditional organization) and showed that these earlier forms cannot achieve efficiency nearly as well, nor was efficiency usually their goal. He understood that although many bureaucracies fall short of these five characteristics, modern organization comes closer to these than traditional organization, and that the drive toward bureaucratization was an important source of change throughout modern society.

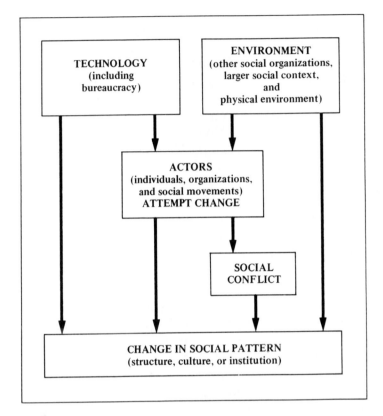

FIGURE 12–3   Technology, Environment, and Social Change

Technology should now be added to our understanding of why change takes place in organization. Note again that like the effects of the outside environment, technology both has direct effects on social organization and has effects through encouraging individuals, organizations, and social movements to attempt change in society with resulting social conflict (see Figure 12–3).

5. CHANGES IN POPULATION CHANGE SOCIAL ORGANIZATION

Numbers matter. As the number of people in an organization grows, there are forces set loose, encouraging change. Population growth in the United States changed the nature of political, economic, and educational institutions. Larger numbers made possible the industrial revolution and rise of urban America. People migrating in large numbers to cities created social problems, which necessitated change. Migrating blacks to southern and then northern cities made the civil rights movement possible in the twentieth century.

Look at your own friendship groups. When there are two people interacting, a certain pattern develops, but as more individuals enter into the group, the pattern changes—we're not always sure how. For example, going to lunch with a friend makes possible the sharing of intimate concerns, but when a third is invited, intimacy is made more difficult.

A business which becomes a large corporation of several thousand employees has problems of coordination, morale, loyalty, and social controls that a business with only three or four employees does not have. Structure changes—for example, a more formal and complex (differentiated) structure is created. Culture changes—efficiency replaces friendship and intimacy as values.

Religious groups, when they are small, have a simple structure and a shared culture which exerts strong controls on the individual and encourages emotional ties. But as the religious groups become larger, not everyone knows everyone else by name, people must be formally elected to positions of leadership, emotional ties weaken, the structure and culture changes, and the group becomes a formal organization.

Small towns become big towns, and big towns become cities or metropolitan centers. Urban life alters society's occupational structure, its class system, and minority-dominant group relations. Urban life alters the relationship between men and women, giving the latter greater opportunity to succeed in the economic and political order. Urban life brings a change in our leisure activities, our level of education, our ideas and values. Urbanization brings problems of transportation, law enforcement, education, health, and government that cannot be dealt with through the traditional ways that characterize a small town. Problems bring solutions; solutions bring new institutions and changing culture.

Formality, complexity, and centralization are tendencies that accompany increasing size (including the large church, the large business, the large urban center). It is difficult to rely on informal controls and face-to-face interaction to achieve organizational goals.

Increasingly, people come to know the organization through written documents—laws, job descriptions, procedures. Complexity also accompanies size: This simply means that there are more status positions added, both in terms of rank levels (vertical) and also in terms of division of labor (horizontal). Not only is there a manager, but now there is also an assistant manager and a part-time assistant manager for evening hours. Not only are there salespeople, but each specializes in a slightly different item. Finally, size also brings the tendency for centralization of decision making: Coordination of large numbers tends to bring the need for fewer and fewer people making more and more of the important decisions.

Because this chapter is necessarily brief, our discussion here cannot consider the reasons for increasing size. Rising birth rates, lower death rates, movements of people from one place to another (migration), and increasing industrialization are some causes which come to mind. However, for purposes of simplicity, we are here pointing out that population change itself is an important cause of social change.

6. CHANGE IN SOCIAL PATTERNS CAUSES CHANGE IN OTHER SOCIAL PATTERNS

Institutions are part of social organization. They are the legitimate procedures established to deal with the problems of society. Although institutions are changed by all the forces described above, they are also independent sources of change. As the institution of marriage changes, for example, or the public school, or the modern corporation, or the American presidency, many other patterns in American life also change. We might think of the effects of institutions as follows:

1. As an institution changes, so do other institutions, since institutions are interrelated. As television becomes more and more important, public schools, political campaigning, and the socialization of children are altered considerably.

2. As institutions change, so do other aspects of culture, such as norms, values, goals, and truths. As professional sports become more central to society, competition and striving to be number one become more important values. Also, the belief that leisure should be directed at watching others perform becomes more accepted.

3. As institutions change, so does social structure. Changes in the institution of marriage alters the relationship between men and women; changes in governmental taxation makes people more or less equal in society.

4. As institutions change in society, smaller levels of social organization are affected: communities, formal organizations, groups, dyads. Bureaucratization in society influences individual formal organizations to become increasingly bureaucratic. Increasing legitimation of divorce in society (a developing institution) affects individual marital dyads.

For many sociologists the most important institutions are economic. Feudalism and capitalism are economic institutions, and as Western society moved from one to the other, maximizing profit replaced subsistence, planning replaced spontaneous effort, modern ways replaced traditional ways, and a drive toward increased consumption of goods influenced the development of a rising middle class and an urban labor force.

Changing culture also influences change. A classical analysis of how culture influences structure was made by Max Weber in *The Protestant Ethic and the Spirit of Capitalism* (1905). Here Weber argued that the development of a Protestant religious philosophy (a set of truths, values, norms, and goals) was instrumental to the development of a capitalist-oriented middle class in Europe. This middle class in turn transformed many European societies into capitalist economic systems. Weber showed that a certain kind of Protestantism (represented in the United States by the Puritans) taught such things as the *value* of hard work, the *truth* that success in this life was proof of election by God for salvation, and the *norm* that people should save and reinvest what they earn. This culture, Weber pointed out, encouraged the development of a hard-working capitalist class, which changed the economic institutions and the structure of society.

And changes in social structure affect culture too. Marx argued this most clearly. Since the culture is produced by those who are most powerful in society, as class changes, the culture will also. Thus, Marx pointed out, as the capitalist class replaced the feudal lords as the dominant class in society, it was their values, their ideas, their norms, and their goals that became dominant in society. We might also point to the occupational structure of the United States to understand the effects of structural change. Today our culture is most influenced by the ideas, norms, and values of corporate executives rather than by farmers or small businessmen.

SUMMARY AND CONCLUSION

This chapter has emphasized the complexity of social change. There are many reasons why organization changes, and that has been its focus. Social change—that is, change in social patterns—result from (1) actors attempting change, (2) social conflict, (3) the social and physical environment, (4) technology, (5) population change, and (6) changes in the patterns themselves. We might once again show this in picture form (see Figure 12–4).

FIGURE 12–4   Causes of Social Change

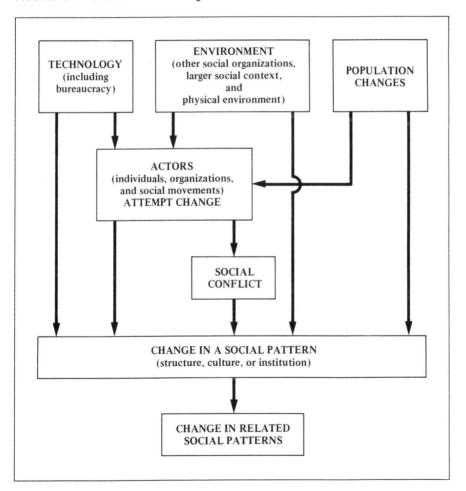

The word "organization" seems to imply continuity and order, but this is misleading. Change and conflict are certainly as much a part of social organization as order and continuity. Organization is always changing, sometimes slightly, sometimes a lot. We all interact and create social patterns, and these patterns become powerful; yet interaction is also dynamic and creates forces for change. Organization is a complex and subtle balance between continuity and change, order and disorder, cooperation and conflict. As Marvin Olsen states in his excellent book on social organization (1978, 4), "All social life [is] a dynamic process of becoming rather than a static state of being."

There is no easy way to understand change. There are many causes of change. Each society's unique social patterns make it difficult to generalize about change between societies. Thus, most sociologists have long given up hoping to find universal laws of social change. Instead, we understand change through isolating tendencies, general directions, and trends.

QUESTIONS TO CONSIDER

1. The author argues that in the long run, the impact of any one individual changing society in his or her image is small. Do you agree? If one holds this view, can he or she still justify trying to change society?

2. What do you think is the most important cause of social change? Is there anything described in this chapter which you believe has little or no effect?

3. What are some of the reasons why understanding social change is so difficult?

RECOMMENDED READING

The following works examine the meaning and causes of social change:

BELL, DANIEL. 1973. *The coming of the post-industrial society.* New York: Basic Books.
BENDIX, REINHARD. 1964. *Nation-building and citizenship.* New York: Wiley.
BERGER, BRIGITTE. 1971. *Societies in change.* New York: Basic Books.
BLUMBERG, PAUL. 1980. *Inequality in an age of decline.* New York: Oxford University Press.
CHIROT, DANIEL. 1986. *Social change in the modern era.* New York: Harcourt Brace Jovanovich.

COSER, LEWIS. 1956. *The functions of social conflict.* Glencoe, Ill.: Free Press.

COTTRELL, W. F. 1951. Death by Dieselization. *American Sociological Review* 16:358–365.

DAHRENDORF, RALF. 1958. Toward a theory of social conflict. *The Journal of Conflict Resolution* 11:170–183.

DAHRENDORF, RALF. 1959. *Class and class conflict in industrial society.* Stanford, Calif.: Stanford University Press.

DURKHEIM, EMILE. [1893] 1964. The division of labor in society. Trans. George Simpson. New York: Free Press.

FLACKS, RICHARD. 1971. *Youth and social change.* Chicago: Markham.

GALBRAITH, JOHN KENNETH. 1967. *The new industrial state.* Boston: Houghton-Mifflin.

GAMSON, WILLIAM. 1968. *Power and discontent.* Homewood, Ill.: Dorsey Press.

GAMSON, WILLIAM. 1975. *The strategy of social protest.* Homewood, Ill.: Dorsey Press.

GARNER, ROBERTA ASH. 1977. *Social change.* Chicago: Rand McNally College Publishing.

GLICK, PAUL C. 1979. The future of the American family. *Current population reports,* ser. P23, no. 78. Washington, D.C.: United States Bureau of the Census.

GOULDNER, ALVIN. 1954. *Patterns of industrial bureaucracy.* New York: Free Press.

GURR, TED R. 1970. *Why men rebel.* Princeton, N.J.: Princeton University Press.

INKELES, ALEX, and D. H. SMITH. 1974. *Becoming modern.* Cambridge: Harvard University Press.

JONES, L. Y. 1980. *Great expectations: America and the baby boom generation.* New York: Coward, McCann & Geoghegan.

KORNHAUSER, WILLIAM. 1961. *The politics of mass society.* New York: Free Press.

LAUER, ROBERT H. 1971. The scientific legitimation of fallacy: Neutralizing social change theory. *American Sociological Review* 36:881–889.

LAUER, ROBERT H. 1973. *Perspectives on social change.* Boston: Allyn & Bacon.

LENSKI, GERHARD. 1966. *Power and privilege: A theory of social stratification.* New York: McGraw-Hill.

MARX, KARL, and FRIEDRICH ENGELS. [1848] 1963. *The communist manifesto.* Trans. Eden Paul and Cedar Paul. New York: Russell & Russell.

MOORE, WILBERT E. 1974. *Social change.* 2d ed. Englewood Cliffs, N.J.: Prentice-Hall.

OGBURN, WILLIAM F. 1950. *Social change.* New York: Viking.

OLSEN, MARVIN E. 1978. *The process of social organization.* New York: Holt, Rinehart & Winston.

OGBURN, WILLIAM F., and NIMKOFF, MEYER. 1955. *Technology and the Changing Family.* Boston: Houghton Mifflin.

SIMMEL, GEORG. [1902–03] 1950. Metropolis and mental life. In *The sociology of Georg Simmel,* ed. Kurt Wolff, 409–426. Glencoe, Ill.: Free Press.

SKOLNICK, ARLENE, and JEROME SKOLNICK. 1980. *Family in transition.* 3d ed. Boston: Little, Brown.

SMELSER, NEIL J. 1962. *Theory of collective behavior.* New York: Free Press.

TURNBULL, COLIN. 1972. *The mountain people.* New York: Simon & Schuster.

TURNER, RALPH H., and LEWIS M. KILLIAN. 1972. *Collective behavior.* Englewood Cliffs, N.J.: Prentice-Hall.

WAITE, LINDA. 1981. *U. S. women at work.* Washington, D.C.: Population Reference Bureau.

WALLERSTEIN, IMMANUEL. 1974. *The modern world system.* New York: Academic Press.

WEBER, MAX. [1905] 1958. *The Protestant ethic and the spirit of capitalism.* Trans. Talcott Parsons. New York: Scribner's.

WEBER, MAX. [1922] 1957. *Theory of social and economic organization.* Eds. A. M. Henderson and Talcott Parsons. New York: Free Press.

WRONG, DENNIS. 1977. *Population and society.* 4th ed. New York: Random House.

Two Girls in a Field (1882) by Winslow Homer (1836–1910), United States. Cooper-Hewitt Museum, Smithsonian Institution/Art Resource, New York. Gift of Charles Savage Homer. (1912–12–80). Reprinted with permission.

13

The Meaning
and Uses
of Sociology

This book is meant to be one introduction to the discipline and perspective of sociology. It is an attempt by one author to describe what the meaning of sociology is to him.

Throughout this book there has been one dominant theme. Sociology is a perspective which focuses on the social nature of the human being. Other perspectives in social science examine the human being, but not with this central focus. The biologist, the chemist, and the psychologist may say that there is more to human beings than their social nature, and they are, of course, correct. No claim can be made that sociology has the final answer. Instead, like all perspectives, sociologists exaggerate, start with a set of assumptions that seem reasonable (and consistent with known evidence), and go from there trying to get as much mileage as possible through theorizing and testing.

The concepts described in this book create the basic parameters, or outline, of sociology. Instead of simply defining sociology in one simple sentence (for example, "the scientific study of society"), it is better to see sociology as the study of these concepts: socialization, social action, interaction, social patterns, social organization, social structure, culture, institutions, social order, social power, social conflict, and social change—to name the most central.

Throughout this book there has been an attempt to describe some of the ideas that are central to sociology—ideas that should prove important for students understanding the human being. Let us for a moment review these ideas.

Human beings are social and socialized. We are born dependent on others. We survive because of them, we learn how to survive from them, we are socialized by them. Socialization is no small matter. Through socialization we take on the ways of society and become members of society. We learn to control ourselves through the rules and perspective of society, thus making society possible. Through socialization we develop symbols, self, and mind, qualities that make us both human and, to some extent, free. Finally, either because of socialization or because of our nature, humans come to live their whole lives around others, subject to the rules that dominate all social life.

Humans are social actors, we interact, and we create social patterns. As we act around others, they become important influences on what we do. We consider them as we act; we are social actors in almost every situation. Interaction—mutual social action—socializes us, influences our actions and ideas, and, over time, influences the development of social patterns. Social patterns, once created, take on a life of their own, influencing actors in interaction. It is such patterns that form the basis of social organization.

Humans live their lives embedded in social organization. We are in the center of many organizations, most of which we had no part in creating. Dyads, groups, formal organizations, communities, and society are, to some extent, the walls of our imprisonment. Each represents rules that we are expected to follow.

Social structure is an important social pattern in all social organization. It positions each actor, tells each what is expected (role), gives the actor an identity and perspective, distributes power, privilege, and prestige. What we do, what we are, and what we believe is linked to our positions in many social structures.

Society is a system of inequality that includes class, gender, and racial/ethnic group positions. These social structures are far-reaching, they are very hard to change, and they place people in positions which are very important for our whole lives.

All social organization has culture. Culture, too, is a social pattern. It is what people share as they interact: their ideas, values, goals, and norms. Our actions are influenced by what our social organizations teach us. What seems like free choice often turns out to be products of the culture which we have learned.

Institutions are social patterns that exist in society. We are all born into a society that has developed certain ways of doing things. Although these appear to be natural or right, they are always alternatives. Institutions are what we inherit from our ancestors. Societies generally have political, economic, military, kinship, educational, health care, and recreational institutions. Institutions are necessary for the continuation of society; institutions control individual choice.

Social order is necessary for all social organization. Order is achieved through controlling the human being. Control is achieved through social structure, culture, institutions, socialization, feelings of loyalty, and social controls. Social controls include the designation of certain people to be outside the acceptable: the condemnation of some as deviant. The human being is part of a world that demands a certain degree of order and control. Although we all do not conform, and although no one conforms completely, society has many ways it tries to assure conformity. Without order and control, organization would be impossible and the human being would also be impossible.

Social power is part of all human relationships. As people act in relation to one another, they exert resources in order to achieve their will. Some win; some lose. Some influence; some are influenced. In general, sociologists see society as a system of unequal power, usually with an elite in control.

Human beings develop symbols, self, and mind in interaction with others. Symbols, self, and mind are qualities that change our relationship with our environment, including other people. Instead of simply responding to stimuli, instead of simply being conditioned by others, we become active, thinking, self-directing, problem-solving, free beings. These qualities are central to what we are; they also are qualities which we develop only through our interaction.

Social organization is always in the process of change. It is easy to get lost in the permanence of organization; in fact, change is as much a part of organization as permanence and stability. There is no one reason organization changes. Change is complex and many-faceted.

These are the core ideas contained in this introduction. Sociology is exciting because of these ideas. If taken seriously, many of these ideas challenge the taken-for-granted truths that many people hold. If taken seriously, these ideas can show us aspects of the human being we have never really considered.

Of course, sociology is also a discipline that has accumulated lots of facts. There are textbooks filled with these facts. There are scientific journals filled with studies of the human being never mentioned in this short introduction. Remember that the purpose here is to introduce the core; if you are interested in more, then investigate further.

THE USES OF SOCIOLOGY

Why study sociology? Consider the following.

First, some students are attracted to sociology as a major or minor field of study. It is interesting, challenging, and applicable to the kinds of questions that concern them. Sometimes sociology becomes a bridge to an appealing occupation. It prepares the individual for many diverse occupations through teaching social research skills, making one sensitive to organizational and interactional patterns, and through providing a body of knowledge that can be applied to almost any occupation that involves working with people.

Knowing sociology contributes to understanding; it contributes to being an educated person. To those who regard truth as an important value, who believe that there is nothing more exciting than understanding self, others, society, and humanity, then sociology is important to study and know.

Sociology can be applied to one's own life. It helps the individual understand why people around him or her act the way they do. It aids an understanding of one's own identity, thinking, and action. It also can be applied to understanding all the organizations of which we are a part and can be useful for achieving our goals in these organizations.

Sociology is liberating; it is a step toward having more control over one's life. We are social beings, and from the beginnings of our lives we have been socialized by family, friends, teachers, and others. Much of what we know we have not scrutinized very carefully. The sociological perspective at the very least exposes the culture and the nature of society to the individual, making it possible to understand oneself more carefully, and to realize that to make choices is to be able to step back and look objectively at the control by our various social organizations.

Not all of us will be affected the same way by sociology. Some of us will find it liberating. Hopefully, sociology will make us more tolerant of human differences, and it will foster a commitment in us to better the human condition. I have taught it for fifteen years, and I still do not know if it has had significant impact on the lives of my students. What I do know, however, is that learning sociology has altered my life considerably. It has been much more than a job for me. It has affected the ideas I use to approach my world. It has given me at least the following insights:

1. To be different is not to be wrong. Social organization, other people in interaction with me, may think me funny or immoral or dumb, but my strangeness is part of their social definition only.

2. We are prisoners in social organization. Much of what we do is determined by the structures and cultures where we are located. Yet there is something liberating about this knowledge—it is one step in making choice, it is one step in living something approaching a free existence. Peter Berger makes this point in *Invitation to Sociology* (1963): Sociology can provide one with an understanding of the rules of the game, the roles we are assigned—and this knowledge is the first step to consciously playing the roles, dealing with those more powerful than we are, and determining our own action in the face of others' rules.

3. Berger underlines another idea that I have found in sociology—things are not what they seem to be. We are cultural animals;

our views of the world are a result of socialization, so that what most of us regard as just "common sense" has been transmitted to us by our groups. Sociology has made me realize that superficial explanations do not constitute understanding—there is a passion for understanding life that sociology has helped me develop.

4. Sociology has made me more realistic about what is possible in society. On the one hand I know that social change is inevitable. One cannot wish change away; and one must come to deal with it both in the larger society and in one's own personal existence. And I have also become less impatient about what I think America can become. I still have ideals that I feel are worth working for, but I have also come to terms with what can realistically be expected, given the power of social structure, culture, institutions, socialization, social controls, and people's loyalties.

If we think not about ourselves as individuals but about the society at large, there are good justifications for a perspective like sociology, a science of society. It is vitally important to study human beings objectively and to make conclusions not on what the world should be like but on what it is like. There should be financial support for sociological research so that we can more fully understand action and also avoid the kinds of problems that ignorance leads to. It is better to know than to be ignorant, and it is better to know about human beings and society scientifically so that we do not have to accept the word of those who "seem" to know what they are talking about—usually they turn out to be people who agree with us. Finally, sociology has something to offer policy makers, not in telling them what to do, but in helping them understand what will happen if, for example, schools remain segregated, or family life becomes increasingly diverse, or the government does or does not regulate television, addictive drugs, or health care. Sociologists have made important contributions to America's consciousness in race relations, poverty, crime, sex roles, and family life. This consciousness may not be a comfortable one, but it is absolutely necessary if we are not to live with myths all of our lives.

Sociology is promising—it offers the learner much. If you are still interested, come back to it. Think of this book as only a beginning, a core, a brief encounter, an invitation.

QUESTIONS TO CONSIDER

1. Describe the meaning of sociology to someone who does not understand it.
2. Describe the sociological view of the human being to someone who does not understand it.
3. Describe the meaning of social organization to someone who does not understand it.

RECOMMENDED READING

The following works are interesting introductions to sociology. You will probably find them more difficult than this introduction.

BERGER, PETER L. 1963. *Invitation to sociology: A humanistic perspective.* Garden City, N.Y.: Doubleday.
INKELES, ALEX. 1964. *What is sociology?* Englewood Cliffs, N.J.: Prentice-Hall.
MILLS, C. WRIGHT. 1959. *The sociological imagination.* New York: Oxford University Press.
OLSEN, MARVIN E. 1978. *The process of social organization.* New York: Holt, Rinehart & Winston.
WEBER, MAX. [1909] 1930. *The Protestant ethic and the spirit of capitalism.* New York: Scribner's.

Index